CHAPEL OF THE
TRANSFIGURATION

"Prayer is the effort of the soul to reach God."

– Mother Foundress Eva Mary, C.T.

CHAPEL OF THE TRANSFIGURATION

Community of the Transfiguration
Cincinnati, Ohio

Chapel of the Transfiguration - Glendale, Ohio

The Community of the Transfiguration wishes to acknowledge
the following assistance in the publication of this book:

Design	Barbara Matulionis
Photography	Greg Matulionis
Editorial/Writing	Jo Anne Moser Gibbons

Community of the Transfiguration
495 Albion Avenue
Cincinnati, Ohio 45246

Published 2002. First edition.
Printed in the United States of America

ISBN 0-9719931-0-6

CONTENTS

ILLUSTRATIONS

All photography is the work of Greg Matulionis, except items marked "archives" in parentheses following the description. Those items are from the archives of the Community of the Transfiguration, Glendale, Ohio.

✠

To the Glory of
God

ACKNOWLEDGMENTS

Open to me the gates of righteousness,
that I may enter through them
and give thanks to the Lord.
This is the Lord's doing,
it is marvelous in our eyes.
This is the day that the Lord has made;
let us rejoice and be glad in it.
O give thanks to the Lord, for he is good,
for his steadfast love endures forever.
(Psalm 118:19, 23, 24, 29)

The Chapel of the Transfiguration is a sacred gift from God – a gift that has been and is cherished by all who "enter the gates." For more than seventy years, people have entered through the doors of the Chapel to pray, to listen, and to be in the presence of God.

For Mother Eva Mary and Sister Beatrice Martha, the building of the Chapel was a call from God to which they responded with prayer, love, and hope. The first gift for the Chapel was an offering from a small Bethany Home child. Many other gifts followed, from families, friends, and strangers, to provide a Chapel for the glory of God and a holy place for all to come.

The Sisters are grateful for Sister Mariya Margaret and the many Sisters who, through the years, have faithfully recorded the history of the Chapel, and to Sister Mary Veronica for her careful research and compilation of the story. We also thank our friends, Associates, and Sisters who, through their love of the Chapel, have generously given their time and gifts for the writing of this book.

We extend our sincere appreciation to Greg Matulionis for his masterful photography, to Barbara Matulionis for her beautiful book design, and to Jo Anne Moser Gibbons for her expert editing and writing. Their sensitivity to and reverence for the Chapel, as well as their creative and artistic abilities, are reflected in this book.

We also thank Helen Haberstroh for allowing us to reproduce her fine drawing of the Chapel, which appears on the title page, and to Elizabeth Maye, whose calligraphic art has been reproduced on several pages of the book.

It is the prayer of the Sisters of the Transfiguration that all who "enter the gates" may behold the King in His beauty and may be blessed and transfigured by this King of glory – for "this is the Lord's doing."

Lift up your heads, O gates!
and be lifted up, O ancient doors!
that the King of glory may come in.
Who is this King of glory?
The Lord of hosts,
he is the King of glory.
(Psalm 24:7, 10)

The Sisters of the Transfiguration
2002

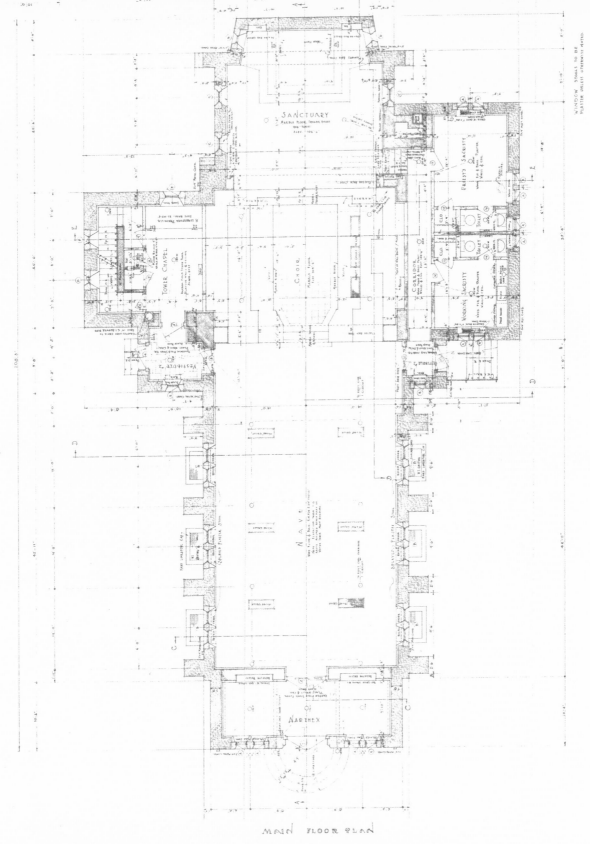

SANCTUARY

PRIEST'S SACRISTY

TOWER CHAPEL

CORRIDOR

WORKING SACRISTY

CHOIR

VESTIBULE 2

NAVE

NARTHEX

MAIN FLOOR PLAN

CRAM AND FERGUSON ARCHITECTS

248 BOYLSTON ST · BOSTON MASS·

O Lord, I love the house in which you dwell,

and the place where your glory abides.

(Psalm 26:8)

Since the day of its consecration in 1929, these sentiments have been echoed by countless people, moved by the beauty of the Chapel of the Transfiguration. Most have come to worship, some just to admire, all to be touched by the prayers, the peace, and the quiet joy that seem to permeate its very stones.

This is the story of how this exquisite Chapel, located on the grounds of the Community of the Transfiguration near Cincinnati, Ohio, came to be, as well as a guide to the Chapel itself and its many objects of beauty and special interest.

This is the story of religious pioneers: Mother Eva Mary, a sensitive, persistent woman whose faith, ideals, and devotion began the Community of the Transfiguration and its more than one hundred years of prayer and service; Sister Beatrice Martha, an inspired and inspiring believer whose vision and guidance, after thirty years, made the dream of the Chapel come true; and the many Sisters of the Transfiguration who lived – and continue to live every day – the spirit of gracious kindness, simplicity, and joy that marks this Episcopal religious order of women.

This is the story of faith, brought to fruition by the graciousness of God and with the help of religious leaders, family members, Associates, and friends who generously supported – and continue to support – the Community's life and ministry.

This is the never-ending story of the continual flow of God's grace and more than a century of prayer and service.

BEGINNINGS

Then I heard the voice of the Lord saying,
"Whom shall I send, and who will go for us?"
And I said, "Here am I; send me!"

(Isaiah 6:8)

In April, 1851, the Cincinnati, Hamilton, and Dayton Railroad was nearly complete. Only scattered settlements remained of the once bustling construction camps along the right of way. Before construction began, a 600-acre subdivision was laid out for railroad officials, owners, and operators of the enterprises starting to develop in the Mill Creek Valley, a mile-wide strip of industrial land running north-south through Cincinnati and nearby communities. This subdivision eventually became the Village of Glendale. It seemed like an expansive park, with winding country roads, streams, and large trees. The ground was also high enough to prevent being affected by the flooding of the nearby Mill Creek. While the area seemed pastoral and untouched by industry, access to the railroad provided residents with fast and convenient transportation to the growing city of Cincinnati just fifteen miles away.

Thomas Stanley Matthews (1824-1889), an attorney for the CH&D Railroad, and an original member of the Glendale Association, bought five acres of land to build a home. In 1854, he and his wife, Mary Ann Black Matthews (1823-1885), and their small family moved into Oakencroft, their new, stately home at 125 East Fountain Avenue. This gracious residence would remain in the family for almost 150 years, until 1993 (see fig. 1.1).

The young couple joined into the life of the village. During the same year that the Matthews moved to Oakencroft, Stanley Matthews established a private law practice and started his political career as one of the original trustees of the Village of Glendale, and later, mayor. They attended the Presbyterian Church, now known as the First Presbyterian Church, Glendale. Then, early in 1859, tragedy struck. In one month, four of the six Matthews children died of scarlet fever. Only seven-year-old Isabella and baby William Mortimer survived the epidemic. Later, in 1868, Isabella died at the age of sixteen.

It is difficult to imagine how parents endure this kind of personal disaster, but somehow, through their faith, the bereaved Stanley and Mary found the strength to go on. Within a few years, their family included four more children: Jane (Mrs. Horace Gray) (1860-1949), Eva (1862-1928), Grace (Mrs. Harlan Cleveland) (1864-1933), and Paul (1866-1954).

Eva Lee Matthews was born in the Fountain Avenue home on February 9, 1862. Stanley Matthews was serving as a lieutenant colonel with his Civil War regiment, the Twenty-Third Ohio Volunteers Infantry, and did not meet his new daughter and eighth child for three months.

The future foundress of the Community of the Transfiguration became part of a home life steeped in literature, music, and the humanities. The children's religious training began in their mother's bedroom. Here they gathered around the fire early every morning to have a happy, social time as they were read Bible stories and recited favorite passages. On Sundays, before the family went off to church, their father took over these morning gatherings.

Eva's idealism and colorful imagination, tempered by a down-to-earth practicality, blossomed during her childhood (see fig. 1.2). In the biography of her beloved older sister, Grace Matthews Cleveland tells of young Eva's overflowing joyfulness and of her dread of reaching the years of "accountability," when she feared life's responsibilities would eliminate childhood happiness. Her siblings were her "cherished playmates, their childish lives made one long fairy tale by her poetic and dominant imagination." (Cleveland 1929, 13)

For their enjoyment, Eva orchestrated hours of "let's pretend" to enact new adventures and ideas that she had conjured. She read them tales, and also wrote many stories, often serial, that she then read to them. Eva further tapped her literary talent by writing verses, sometimes co-authored by her mother, to whom she was quite close. Her taste for good reading was nurtured

Fig. 1.1
Oakencroft – Glendale, Ohio
Birthplace of Mother Eva Mary

Fig. 1.2
Eva Lee Matthews at an Early Age

Fig. 1.3
Paul and Eva Matthews (1886)

first at home in the family's library of about 2,000 works, where Sir Walter Scott, Charles Dickens, William Thackeray, and Elizabethan poets became Eva's personal favorites.

From even her earliest childhood years, Eva Matthews was a gifted storyteller, full of imagination and an eye for nuances of character. Her letters from a trip to England, Scotland, and Europe in 1875 with her father and elder sister Jane reflect an early talent for observing and recording detail, communicating important insights, and spinning fascinating tales that would one day delight the children of Bethany Home.

According to her sister Grace, Eva was by nature ardent and intense, introspective and sensitive. Frequently impatient, in her earlier years she was known to exhibit a sudden and unexpected temper.

At the age of thirteen, Eva joined the Presbyterian Church. Soon after, she found herself involved in a difficult, intellectual struggle between Protestant and Catholic principles. Eva would continue to seek answers for well over a decade, including experiments with fasting and prayer as a means to holy living (Cleveland 1929, 26).

In 1877, when Stanley Matthews was appointed to the United States Senate from Ohio, the Matthews family moved to a townhouse in Washington, DC, keeping Oakencroft as their country retreat. There, as a teenager, Eva availed herself of the libraries, languages, and travel she had learned to love. She spent 1881 and part of 1882 at Wellesley College in Massachusetts, whose library furthered her study of languages, modern and ancient. In a letter to her mother, Eva says: "I feel most the value of a fine education when I am in a library, and in a somewhat less degree when I am studying the ancient languages, in both of which – Latin and Greek – I am very much interested…. We hoard every minute of our time to spend in the library." (Cleveland 1929, 21) She was also greatly interested in French, German, and Spanish.

In 1882, due to Eva's delicate health, she left Massachusetts and returned home to Washington. The year before, President James Garfield had appointed Senator Matthews to the Supreme Court, a post he would retain until his death in 1889. Politics, prestige, and the whirling social life of the nation's capital had little appeal for Justice Matthews' daughter, but she did enjoy travel. Accompanied by her aunt, Eva spent the spring of 1883 in Paris studying French and enjoyed living with a French family.

Their trip was cut short by urgent word from Eva's mother, Mary, to return home because of the serious illness of Eva's younger brother, Paul. During the long period of nursing him back to health, Mary's own health began to fail, and she died two years later.

Her death devastated the entire family. Greatly affected by this personal loss and his return to health, Paul felt that his life had been given back at a great price and was no longer his own. Foregoing a law career, he entered Princeton Theological Seminary with the intent of becoming a Presbyterian minister.

At the age of twenty-three, Eva experienced some of her darkest moments following her mother's death. It was an occasion for deep soul-searching and coming to peace with her own religious faith, including belief in the communion of saints and prayers for the departed (Cleveland 1929, 26, 42).

Following her mother's death, Eva's own health began to fail. As a result, fall, 1885 found Eva in Princeton, where her father had sent her to be with Paul (see fig 1.3). His intent was to help Eva regain her spirituality and health while she struggled to accept both her mother's death and her father's remarriage soon thereafter. At Princeton, she was able to find time to learn and read Hebrew and Greek while keeping house for Paul, until he left in 1888 for

General Theological Seminary in New York City, where he was confirmed in the Episcopal Church.

The bond between Eva and Paul grew even stronger during this time, and it would remain stable and strong throughout her life. Her brother's influence and guidance in the coming years had a profound effect on Eva Matthews' vocation and the development of the Community of the Transfiguration.

Eva then spent some time back at Oakencroft, where younger sister Grace, newly married, was now living with her husband. In December, 1888, she returned to Washington to nurse her ill father, who died on March 22 of the following year. Her precious spare time there was spent in ministry with Associated Charities and with the Presbyterian Church of the Covenant in that city.

Spending the winter of 1890 in Oxford, England with her younger brother, Eva Matthews came to fully accept the Anglo-Catholic belief with which she had been struggling for so long. During that time, Eva and Paul spent many hours discussing their faith, as she wrote to her sister Grace:

> … I am slowly becoming convinced that he is right and I am wrong; but the more convincing his arguments are, the more rebellious I grow. I do not want to believe – I ought to be ashamed to say it – I am afraid of the consequences of believing. (Cleveland 1929, 38)

Apparently the Good Friday Vigil of that year brought the certainty she needed. On her return to Glendale in the spring, the Right Reverend Boyd Vincent, Bishop of Southern Ohio, confirmed Eva Lee Matthews in the Episcopal Church.

At the time, the Episcopal Church was confronting serious challenges in its attempt to serve the faithful. Many of its small mission churches were barely surviving due to financial and staffing problems. Members of these parishes were often poor, with large families that needed material help as well as spiritual guidance and religious training. As a practical way to meet the need of struggling urban and suburban parishes for clergy, the Episcopal Church established Associate Missions, a semi-monastic movement, throughout the United States.

In 1891, the Reverend Paul Matthews, ordained to the priesthood that year, and his sister Eva joined the Associate Mission way of life in Omaha, Nebraska (see fig. 1.4). The Reverend Irving Peake Johnson, Paul's lifelong friend who was ordained at the same time, was already there. He would become not only Eva's close friend, but also spiritual advisor and helpmate in the future development of the Community of the Transfiguration. Both men had offered their services to the Episcopal Church for three years of parish work.

Fig. 1.4
Parochial School of the Associate Mission
Omaha, Nebraska

Fig. 1.5
Beatrice McCobb Henderson

Here, among the many challenges of Omaha life, the vocation of Eva Matthews would be nurtured and grow. Her organizational skills, her sensitivity to the needs of young children, and her concern for women's intellectual lives were forged for her greater work, yet to come. Here she also developed her keen awareness of single women's need for meaningful work outside the home – the impetus for some of her future Community's ministries.

Now twenty-nine years old, Eva poured herself into the busy life in Omaha. She did the housekeeping, organized women's work, and formed a Women's Auxiliary. She did not overlook the social life of youth in the Associate Mission; there were frequently younger voices heard around the piano and interesting discussions with teens and young adults over dinner. Eva further developed her uncanny storytelling ability during this time, which attracted many clergy and friends to her side.

Eva taught Sunday school, brought poor children under her personal care, and attended church services in all parts of Omaha, often during the severe winters and intense summer heat. At the end of the first year, she wrote: "What joy I have found in this full, rich life of service that the Church is ever offering!" (Cleveland 1929, 64)

Eva's chance meeting with fifteen-year-old Beatrice McCobb Henderson at a Baptismal service changed the lives of both. In the years ahead, this young woman would become Eva's partner in the development of the Community. Born on April 12, 1877 in Lake Forest, Illinois, Beatrice was baptized at the age of six by a Congregational minister. Beatrice's family moved to Omaha, where she refused to attend the local Presbyterian church. Her mother, who was the organist at the Mission church, took her along to services to keep her from "growing up as the heathen" (Cleveland 1929, 81). Beatrice attended Father Irving Johnson's religion classes at the Associate Mission and became interested in Episcopal teachings. Bishop George Worthington confirmed her in the Episcopal Church in a private service on the Eve of Saint John Baptist Day, June 24, 1894, in St. Augustine's Chapel in Hanscom Park, Nebraska.

Joining Eva, Beatrice became involved in the Mission's ministry. She was responsible for taking care of the Mission's dining room and, with every member of the house assigned a church, Beatrice taught Sunday school and became a godmother to many of the children (see fig. 1.5).

During the Omaha years, Eva began investigating religious communities. Becoming more sure of her vocation, she contacted the Sisters of St. Monica for Widows in Fond du Lac, Wisconsin, who worked among the abandoned women of the area. The Sisterhood of St. Mary in Peekskill, New York, also appealed to her. She made a retreat in their Chicago house and became an Associate.

It was to the sisterhood that Eva looked for the realization of cloistered life and vows. In these communities and others she visited, Eva found women leading quiet, happy lives in and out of the cloister with varied work in many areas. Eva said of this searching time: "I believe it to be God's will clearly intimated to me that I should enter a convent and lead a cloistered life." (Cleveland 1929, 78)

Her family thought otherwise, and pressured Eva not to make this decision. Paul and Grace were "against her entering one of the established sisterhoods of the Church. They dreaded what they felt would be the inevitable separation." (Cleveland 1929, 81)

While these personal battles raged in Eva's mind and heart, life in Omaha continued to keep her active, involved, and focused, and the lives of Beatrice and Eva crossed more than ever. Eva was Beatrice's French teacher and became a special influence in Beatrice's life. As Sister Beatrice later explained: "Learning from her was only pleasure. I cannot explain just what the influence

was, for we seldom got off the subject of the lesson, and I saw her only in class, but that she was my guiding star and my ideal from my first lesson, I do know." (Cleveland 1929, 82) Meanwhile, Beatrice did secretarial work for the Women's Auxiliary.

Then, with the help of the Associate Mission, Eva developed a "house of women" – initially with six women and three girls, one of whom was Beatrice. Keeping a schedule of hours for prayer and a semi-religious life, the women taught school, sewed for the poor, and made guild and mission calls.

Her experience with the house of women led Eva to change her mind about her vocation and the direction of her work within that vocation. She discovered that she could be a leader in a house of women, so she was inclined to respect her brother's wishes that she not join an existing community. But there were still inner forces working against her growing call to found her own community. Not only did she feel presumptuous in thinking she could plan and establish a community when she really knew nothing about it, but she also feared the notoriety and the inevitable criticism, as well as the responsibility.

Eva wavered and struggled. Finally she decided to write the letter of application to the Community of St. Mary. She literally had pen in hand, ready to write the letter, when Father Johnson, who was working at the Mission with Eva and the others, approached her desk. "What are you doing?" he asked.

In what must have been an inspiring moment of spiritual direction and self-discovery, Father Johnson convinced Eva that she was capable of leadership, that the West needed a religious community for women, and that her experience with the Associate Mission had prepared Eva for pioneer religious work (Cleveland 1929, 96).

Later, in the forward of Grace Cleveland's biography of her sister, Father Johnson, now a bishop, seemed to clarify his own perspective about Eva: "It was a perplexing question [Eva] faced. Her humility called her to accept the leadership of existing orders; while her convictions and her love of adventure prompted her to pioneer in creating an order that should preserve that which was excellent in medieval tradition but should add certain elements more adaptable to the genius of the Anglican Church. It was from discussion along these lines that I learned much of that which she wished to accomplish." (Cleveland 1929, ix)

There was now no turning back. Eva's struggle to acknowledge her vocation and the role she would play in her developing religious life was over. She decided that she would found a Community in the Diocese of Southern Ohio and began making plans.

During the summer of 1895, Paul and Eva made an extended pilgrimage to the Holy Land. In their absence, young Beatrice became responsible for the spiritual life of the house of women, seeing that the rule was kept and that spirits were high.

Always alert for the needs of the Community that was forming in her mind, Eva began preparations during this trip for a rule of life and formulated customs for the yet-unborn religious community. She observed the dress of the women of Bethlehem, which later was used as a model for a habit – simple, beautiful, and serviceable. It was here that she chose the Jerusalem Cross as her Community's emblem.

By Easter, 1896, brother Paul and sister Eva were back at Oakencroft, the family estate in Glendale, Ohio, and Paul began his work at Saint Luke Church in nearby Cincinnati. Eva continued her efforts to establish a community. The sanction of the Bishop of the Diocese of Southern Ohio was required, and Bishop Boyd Vincent tried to persuade Eva to become a deaconess instead. When Eva disagreed, he finally allowed her to develop plans for a religious

Fig. 1.6
The First Postulants
Eva Matthews (l.) and Beatrice Henderson

community, but with one provision: she must recognize his authority by obedience to him as her diocesan bishop. To this Eva agreed.

During her visit to the Holy Land, Eva was disappointed to discover that the name she had chosen, "Mary and Martha of Bethany," could not be used. There was already a "Sisterhood of Bethany" in the English Church. When she later consulted with Bishop Vincent, he asked her what her favorite collect was. She told him of her love for the Transfiguration. She wished to make her new Community one distinctly grounded in the Prayer Book tradition, and was aware that the ancient Feast of the Transfiguration was restored in the American 1892 revision of *The Book of Common Prayer.* So Eva Lee Matthews chose this feast for her new American Community. Quietly, she knew that she still had other plans for the use of "Bethany."

In early June, 1896, Eva returned to Omaha to close the household there, then returned to Cincinnati with those women who wanted to participate in her new work. Like many other Associate Missions, the Omaha Associate Mission had stabilized enough to survive on its own and was able to support its own rector. Soon the Associate Missions of the Episcopal Church would be ministries of the past.

Back in Cincinnati, Eva moved to 1711 Freeman Avenue, near Saint Luke Church in the central city, to assist Paul with teaching and parish work. Beatrice Henderson, her mother, and her sister Marian, all of whom had been at the Mission House in Omaha, soon joined Eva. Eva and Beatrice began to live by rule and wore the distinctive dress of postulants (see fig. 1.6)

The Mission House in Cincinnati, developed under the direction of the Reverend Paul Matthews, evolved as a response to the poor physical and environmental conditions for the children in the area. Many families were homeless, and early childhood care was almost unknown. Birth and early infancy mortality rates were high. The women of the Mission House undertook such daily tasks as mothers' meetings for sewing, Bible study and guild work, Sunday school teaching, and visits to children in hospitals. Their work grew so rapidly, overflowing existing space, that second sessions were planned.

These opportunities for local women and children were as much social as spiritual. Beatrice visited children in hospital wards, and they called the nineteen-year-old girl "Mama." She brought them peppermints. Wednesday was Flower Market Day in Cincinnati, and Beatrice would often be sent to buy flowers to distribute to children living in the city's tenements.

The group saw a need to enable city children and their families to breathe fresh country air during the summer heat and thus escape from summertime illnesses. In summer, 1897, Eva sent Beatrice and Nellie Bechtel, one of the Mission House workers, to Glendale to organize and supervise a summer camp for families. For that purpose, she had rented the old Allen homestead on Congress and Fountain avenues from May to October. After six weeks, Ethel Lee (later Sister Ethel Bertha), a member of Eva's Sunday school, replaced Miss Bechtel.

By the end of the summer, it was obvious that several children could not return to their city homes. Now a choice had to be made for the full focus of their work, and the women chose to work with children. The need was great: at the time, most infants in the central city area did not survive beyond seven months due to lack of good early care in their homes. So the women established a children's home next door to the city Mission House with six children whose mothers were not able to provide for them after their summer in the country. The foundation of Bethany Home came from these early days on Freeman Avenue.

It wasn't long before the children's home outgrew its city quarters, and a new location was needed. Glendale seemed to be the right place. In the late 1890s, many Matthews family members continued to live there. It was a natural choice for Eva to place the Community in a familiar locale that still enjoyed the country atmosphere in which she herself thrived. Mortimer Matthews helped his sister purchase property that included a manor house, which became the nucleus of the Community's property in Glendale today. The dwelling had been empty for nearly a decade, so repairs were needed from roof to basement.

But the condition of the house did not deter Beatrice, who first saw it on Saturday, July 2, 1898. On the very next day, she and her entourage moved in. This was in the heat of summer, and Beatrice knew that the very survival of several infants was at stake as she and Ethel Lee packed up the Freeman Avenue house. That morning, the motley group of Mission women, babies, children, and other adults boarded the ten o'clock train to Glendale. Matthews family carriages were waiting at the station to transport them all to the house at 495 Albion Avenue. The babies survived the trip and were put to sleep on the grass. Bethany Home was born!

Fig. 1.7
Bethany Home Children

The group camped out that summer as cleaning, repairs, and the addition of some modern conveniences went on. Beatrice, Ethel Lee, and other helpers assumed responsibility for the daily work at Bethany Home, while many Glendale friends donated food and furnishings. Eva and Beatrice seldom saw each other during these months, as Eva continued to live fifteen miles away in the city Mission House.

Less than a month later, on the Feast of the Transfiguration, August 6, 1898, Eva Lee Matthews and Beatrice McCobb Henderson were admitted as novices into the new Community of the Transfiguration. The three-hour service at Saint Luke Church in Cincinnati was a "command performance" for clergy of the diocese, for Bishop Vincent had much to say on the "sisterhood" life, and he wanted all the clergy to be there. Taking vows of poverty, chastity, and obedience, the two women became known as Sister Eva Mary and Sister Beatrice Martha, with Sister Eva Mary noted as foundress. The Reverend Paul Matthews presented the first two Sisters of the Community to Bishop Vincent.

On the Eve of Transfiguration Day, August 5, 1898, the first seven Associates were admitted. This group, which then, as now, supported the Community in so many ways, today embraces hundreds of people from around the world.

Soon after these momentous occasions, Sister Eva and Sister Beatrice traveled to Hickory Nut Gap, North Carolina for a much needed rest. There, in the mountains, the Community's missionary work in that area first came into being.

Bishop Vincent blessed the property in Glendale on St. Michael and All Angels Day, September 29, 1898 and Bethany Home was formally opened (see fig. 1.7). Sister Eva's brother Paul preached the sermon. He took his text from 2 Corinthians 3:18: "And all of us, with unveiled faces, seeing the glory of the Lord as though reflected in a mirror, are being transformed into the same image from one degree of glory to another; for this comes from the Lord, the Spirit."

After a five-year novitiate, which was a time for testing, trial, and probation as much for the neophyte Community as for its first two members, Sister Eva Mary made her life vows on August 6, 1903 and assumed the executive position of Mother Superior. She served in this capacity until her death twenty-five years later. For her own personal reasons, Sister Beatrice chose to make her profession at a later time: Ash Wednesday, March 8, 1905 (see fig. 1.8). She chose Ash Wednesday "so there could be no festivities." (Beatrice 1940, 100)

The story of the Chapel of the Transfiguration is rooted in these events, which portray the spirit, love, and commitment of the two pioneer women who established the vibrant religious Community of the Transfiguration. From the earliest days, the vision of a Chapel that would be the center of life for the Community of the Transfiguration and Bethany Home was never far from the imagination of the two founding Sisters. During their trip to England in 1907 to visit and study religious communities, Mother Eva and Sister Beatrice were already acquiring art works and other items for the English Village Gothic Chapel of their dreams, even though actual construction would not begin for another two decades.

✠

Fig. 1.8
Mother Eva Mary and
Sister Beatrice Martha as
Life Professed Sisters

Since the very beginning of the Community and Bethany Home in 1898, the Sisters and children together have worshiped God. Their first chapel was the ballroom of the original house. In 1905, the chapel was enlarged by the addition of a choir and sanctuary. For thirty years, it held the entire family, until they overflowed into the hall and up the stairway. It is incredible the number of people it held – children, friends, Associates, and Sisters of the Transfiguration. Soon it was realized, though, that no corner of the house or the chapel that extended from it would accommodate the many Sisters whom God would send and the children they would care for. So, though they loved the little chapel, the Sisters hoped for a building made especially for the glory and worship of God.

The dream started to become real with the opening of the Chapel Fund in 1906, thanks to a one-dollar donation. The generous and memorable donor was Ella Myers (later Sister Eleanor Mary) who, with her sister Anna (later Sister Anna Grace), were numbers sixteen and seventeen of the first Bethany Home girls. Ella's contribution initiated a stream of donations of pennies, nickels, dimes, and quarters from other Bethany Home girls and from the Sisters.

These hard-earned contributions came from countless sales and projects. Articles of embroidered garments, tooled leather pieces, and woodcarvings were made and sold. Especially popular, too, were items made from exquisite Venetian beads, brought from Paris by a sister of Mother Eva just for this purpose. The woodcarvings were made with the help of Sister Clara Elizabeth, a Swiss native and expert woodcarver. A Convent culinary specialty, homemade marmalade, was a successful sale item for many years. Every year, Christmas offerings were added to the fund. Mrs. Walter St. John Jones, the first person outside the Community to donate, gave the first large gift: $420. Two subsequent gifts of $5,000 each helped greatly.

With contributions small and large, the Chapel Fund began to grow. By 1927, there was enough money assured to build the Chapel, but the Sisters always said: "The first $1,000 was the hardest!"

In fall, 1907, Mother Eva and Sister Beatrice left for England on a cattle boat, designed to prevent seasickness in cattle. They found out that the design also worked well for humans! At Mother Eva's insistence, they traveled through England, Scotland, and Wales in third class railroad accommodations as pilgrims and tourists. The two women visited Anglican religious communities, cathedrals, and churches, always seeking guidance and ideas for their new Community.

Before World War I, it was customary for Americans traveling abroad to buy large pieces of art, usually copies, for their homes and churches. This trip enabled the Sisters to begin purchasing a number of beautiful works of art with religious themes that would fill the walls of the Chapel.

The story is told of their decision to purchase a massive copy of *John the Baptist with Lamb* by Bartolome Murillo. In a letter home, Mother Eva writes that, when they first saw it, she "had pretty nearly committed [to] the extravagance of buying...but fifty guineas!" (Beatrice 1940, 116) (In 1907, that was $250.) Further, in a report home, she somewhat facetiously complains: "I'm afraid we shall never be able to build though, for Sister Beatrice is getting such large ideas that I do not know how she will come down to the day of small things." To keep purchases in perspective, they brought home an alms basin "with Saxon and Celtic designs like

---

Why build a chapel?

In his turn-of-the-century analysis of ecclesiastical architecture, Church Building, Chapel architect Ralph Adams Cram, Ph.D. identified four essential reasons for the existence of church buildings. They point to his ideals of church form and structure – ideals shared by Mother Eva and Sister Beatrice.

First, "a church is a house of God." Thus, he argues, churches must be the finest, the most splendid buildings possible, since they reflect "a visible type of heaven itself."

Second, a church building is a "place apart," the focus of sacramental life. Therefore, everything about the building must be subordinate to the altar, every aspect of the building must point to the altar, and the altar itself must be the finest possible.

Third, the church building must be a harmonious work of art designed to lift human minds to spiritual things "that their souls may be brought into harmony with God."

Fourth, and the least important, says Cram, a church building is one "where a congregation may conveniently listen to the instructions of its spiritual leaders." (Cram 1924)

Fig. 1.9
Altar Photo Shown to
Dr. Ralph Adams Cram

the interweaving of baskets." This they had found at Iona, and at considerably less cost than fifty guineas.

They continued to collect art works and furnishings for the Chapel, still in the planning stages. The Reverend Charles Brookins, the Sisters' chaplain, had received a magnificent oak altar from his son, Arthur Nieb. The beautiful altar carvings depict Jesus blessing little children, Mary and Martha with Our Lord at Bethany, and Mary washing Christ's feet with ointment.

"What more appropriate [altar] for Bethany Home and our Sisters, especially as the figures of a monk and a nun are carved on the left and right corners?" Sister Beatrice exclaimed. "It truly has been made for our Chapel-to-be!" The Sisters purchased the altar with the help of Associates, and then stored it in the Convent where it awaited its proper place in the Chapel.

In 1927, the time had come. After nearly thirty years of prayers, hopes, dreams, visions and fundraising, the Sisters achieved a momentous milestone in the history of the Chapel at the Boston home of Jane (Mrs. Horace) Gray, Mother Eva's sister.

Ralph Adams Cram, Ph.D. (1863-1942), an authority on medieval architecture, came to tea that afternoon. Architect for the Cathedral of St. John the Divine and planning consultant for the National Cathedral in Washington, D.C., Dr. Cram was architect for the Gothic buildings of Kemper Hall at the Community of St. Mary's school in Kenosha, Wisconsin. He authored several books, including *Church Building*, *The Substance of Gothic*, *The Ministry of Art*, and *Ruined Abbeys of Great Britain*.

Together Mother Eva and Sister Beatrice shared their vision for the Chapel with Dr. Cram. They showed him a photograph of the altar in storage in Glendale (see fig. 1.9). Dr. Cram admired the three carved panels, since he also had a special devotion to these Bethany events, and he was impressed with the fact that it had been acquired some years before in anticipation of its future use. During their discussion, Mother Eva explained that she wanted the Chapel to be cruciform and its architecture to be English Village Gothic. Sister Beatrice showed him the 3 ft. x 3 ft. sketch she had made.

A few days later, the three met at Dr. Cram's office to review his preliminary plans. They so closely matched the Sisters' ideas that he observed: "You must have an architect in your family. There is hardly anything that needs changing!"

The Sisters and the architect were of one mind: a House of God must be as beautiful, as grand, as perfect in every way as they could make it. So enthusiastic was Dr. Cram about the Chapel that he donated his services to the Community. Dr. Cram is said to have exclaimed: "This will be fun!"

The estimated cost, in 1927, for building the Chapel was forty cents per cubic foot or $150,000. Since the consecration of a church can only take place for a debt-free building, construction was not begun until the full amount was nearly raised. Long, hard years of fundraising had made this possible. In addition to financial contributions for the Chapel itself, there had already been many gifts for its furnishings, both to beautify the Chapel and to provide items essential for its use. Mrs. William Cooper Procter provided funds for the largest single gift, the organ, in memory of her sister, Miss Mary H. Johnston.

The Chapel groundbreaking took place on St. Michael and All Angels Day, September 29, 1927. In a letter to Sister Mariya Margaret many years after the groundbreaking service, Izetta Howard Aldenger, a former Bethany Home girl, wrote: "Bishop Matthews dug the first shovel full of dirt for the foundation of the new church. I walked in front of him and carried the shovel in the procession, and I was surely thrilled to have that part in it and to be that close to the Bishop!"

It was a mere twenty-one months from the groundbreaking to the Consecration on June 11, 1929. The building of the Chapel had taken less than two years. Credit for such a feat must be given first of all to Dr. Ralph Adams Cram of Cram and Ferguson Architects, Boston, and the associate architects, Matthews and Dennison of Cincinnati. (Stanley Matthews Cleveland of that firm was the nephew of Mother Eva.) The architectural team selected a superb construction team, headed by Frank G. Hamer. Artisans and workers who were present throughout the entire building program included Otto Kadon, stone worker; D.I. Pomeroy, plasterer; William Lichtenberg, painter; Fred Grote, roofer; Z.T. Taylor, clerk; "Tony," the carpenter; "Lesser," the plumber; and "Tone," the faithful laborer.

Chapel construction began in April, 1928. Its progress was well-noted by the eyewitnesses at the time, who watched the Chapel grow and recorded it in *The Bethany Home Chronicle* (see fig. 1.10).

May, 1928

Though Mother Eva's health had begun to fail, on good days she was able to sit on the balcony of the Convent and watch the foundation take shape. She had long dreamed that the Chapel would rise in the center of the grounds. It should be the center of life for the Community, quiet and comforting and yet with continual impact.

Fig. 1.10
Chapel Construction Underway

July, 1928

It is with a sad heart that we resume our Chronicle – our dear Reverend Mother Eva Mary is with us no longer.... She became weaker, and towards the end of June, it was thought best to take her away from the dampness here to the clearer, dryer air of Colorado, as she was breathing with difficulty. She stood the journey well, but grew worse rapidly after reaching Denver.... She was calm and happy and breathed her last the morning of July 6, 1928.... She was brought home to Glendale and the casket was placed in the choir of the oratory, where the Sisters and girls of Bethany Home kept loving watch until Tuesday morning when a Requiem Mass was celebrated.... The body was placed in the vault of Spring Grove Cemetery, from whence it will be removed to the new church when a place is prepared for it.

September, 1928

Mr. and Mrs. Bullock of Boston have been visiting us. Mr. Bullock is the architect from the office of Ralph Adams Cram who comes to look at the rising Chapel which he is building from Mr. Cram's plans.

September 29, 1928

At the time of the service for the laying of the cornerstone on St. Michael and All Angels Day, there was enough flooring for the Sisters to stand inside its rising walls; the rest of the congregation remained outside.

October, 1928

The Chapel is beginning to show its future beauties and is rising rapidly with very little noise or fuss.

November, 1928

Our Church is heavenward reaching. The stonemasons have nearly completed their task. This is one of the most interesting periods of Bethany Home history.... One can never tire of watching the workers. It seems as if God himself were directing them. Each stone is tested and carried up the scaffold by hand so as not to jar the building. The framework of the rose window is being set up and the tower rises. There is very little noise as most of the building is done by hand.... We hope for the best weather so there will be no delay in the future construction of the wonderful 'House of God'.

December, 1928

The new Church is advancing. The tower is finished. The heavy oak timbers for the roof are in place.... And what material! Douglas fir from Mount Shasta, California, weighing two and a half tons each formed trusses, and the lesser timbers were in proportion.... At last all were assembled and a hoisting and wrecking company's derrick appeared on the grounds. A tremendous apparatus was placed in the center of the Church, and then the thrills of watching these gigantic trusses, now firmly riveted together to form a peak, being hoisted in mid-air, swung around and settling each in its place with such apparent ease. The amazing part is they fitted to an inch in the place appointed for them. And then the hoisting machinery slipped out of the Chapel and was away before we had time to see it go.... But sleet and ice are upon us, and the ribs of our roof rise bleak and bare, like a wrecked ship upturned upon the beach....

January, 1929

We delight in seeing the walls of stone rising, each stone carefully selected and placed. The weather is perfect for building, and the small army of competent stonemasons enabled the walls to rise with amazing swiftness.

January, 1929

The Church is progressing slowly because of the winter storms. The workmen work on fair days. The roof is finished except for the tiling, which will not be put on until later. It is now covered with a temporary tarred paper covering, making it possible to go on with work in the interior. We hope now that the work may progress more rapidly since it can be done under cover.

April, 1929

The Church is coming on rapidly. The scaffolding has been removed both without and within. The glass is in the windows. The slate roof is finished. Several tons of organ pipes are in place. Herr [Fritz] Abplanalp has arrived from Switzerland and the workshop is producing beautiful carved work. Sister Clara and he are working long hours daily with what help others can give.

May, 1929

The Chapel is progressing rapidly. The ground round about it has been cleared and leveled and looks well. Inside the floor men, the marble men, the organ men and others are rushing their work to completion for all must be ready by June eleventh. Generous friends have given bells and we are now hoping to have a complete carillon of twenty-five bells. These will not be ready for some months but we hope to hear them next Christmas Eve at midnight.

OUR CHAPEL WALLS, NOW BUILDING

Swift and sure,

Yet to endure,

They are rising high toward heaven.

Each stone set,

Carefully met.

Fitted, placed, as gem engraven.

Glory rings,

As chisel sings.

Oh, Christ our Lord, accept the praises!

High and strong,

Their time prolong.

Here God be loved throughout all ages.

– Sister Beatrice

The Chapel was indeed completed on schedule and ready for the Service of Consecration on the Feast of Saint Barnabas, June 11, 1929. Only the completion of the extensive carvings by Fritz Abplanalp, which would continue for another six years, and the creation and installation of the stained glass windows remained.

The Chapel was ready to assume its place at the center of the life of the Community of the Transfiguration and Bethany Home, as Mother Eva had hoped.

In addition to fulfilling its role as the place of daily worship for the Sisters and Bethany Home and Bethany School children, the Chapel has been the setting for a wide variety of events, ranging from quiet, individual prayer to the majestic splendor of special occasions.

Laying of the Cornerstone

September 29, 1928 seemed an especially appropriate occasion for the Service of Laying the Cornerstone, since it was Saint Michael and All Angels Day, the patronal feast of Bethany Home and Bethany School and the anniversary of the blessing of the Home by Bishop Vincent in 1898. The service began in the Convent chapel, now to be known as the oratory, where Bishop Paul Matthews, the Reverend Gerald Lewis (chaplain), visiting clergy, visitors, children, Associates, and Sisters were assembled.

After the invocation, prayers, and responses, Psalm 122 was read: "I was glad when they said to me, 'Let us go to the house of the Lord!'" The "Transfiguration Hymn," which begins "Lord, it is good for us to be here on the holy mount with Thee," was sung, followed by an address by Bishop Matthews entitled "Living Stones." His text was Ephesians 2:19-22. The Reverend Gilbert P. Symons then read Psalm 127: "Unless the Lord builds the house, those who built it labor in vain." A procession formed, and everyone, with the children carrying banners, marched to the new Chapel singing "The Church's One Foundation."

Fig. 1.11
Cornerstone of Chapel of the Transfiguration

Contents of the Cornerstone Box

crucifix

Jerusalem Cross pin

manuscript of Mother Eva's life

Living Church

Denver newspaper

Witness

Spirit of Missions

four pictures of Bethany Home

Prayer Book and Hymnal

The Holy Bible

letter from Judge Matthews

Genesis and Evolution
by Mother Eva

Manual of Associates

Short Studies in the Book of Job

*Rule of the Community of
the Transfiguration*

Little Pilgrimage to the Holy Land
by Mother Eva

photograph of Mother Eva

photograph of Sister Beatrice

photograph of
Bishop Matthews

report of the works of
the Community

an 1898 penny

report of Bethany Home
and Benediction Service

Bethany Chronicle

*For all publications,
one copy was enclosed.*

Fig. 1.13
The Chapel of the Transfiguration – 1929

The Chapel was far enough along to show its future beauties. A partial floor allowed the Sisters to stand inside the rising walls, while others stood on the ground outside. The Bishop spread the mortar, then the cornerstone (see fig. 1.11), containing a copper box 6 in. x 6 in. x 10 in. that held almost two dozen items, was lowered into place. The Service closed with prayers for the future of the building and its influence for good, for the Community, for children, and for the safety and guidance of the builders and workmen. The recessional hymn was "O 'twas a joyful sound to hear."

That same day, Sister Beatrice was installed as Mother Superior, a position to which the Community had elected her following Mother Eva's death in July, 1928 (see fig. 1.12).

Consecration of the Chapel

It was June, 1929, and, amazingly, the Chapel was nearing completion on schedule (see fig. 1.13). Last-minute details were being completed and laborers were working overtime, but it still seemed to Sister Beatrice that the bare building could not possibly be ready for the consecration celebrations. So that they could get used to the feel of it, she began to bring the

Fig. 1.12
Mother Beatrice Martha

children in to visit the building while it still was full of scaffolding and workmen were finishing the floors (see. fig. 1.14). So much remained to be done that she was "nearly discouraged," as she related in a wonderfully warm letter to fellow Sisters who were unable to attend. (All the following statements attributed to Sister Beatrice are excerpted from that inspiring, lengthy letter, which provides rich details that seem to make the festivities come alive again almost seventy-five years later.)

But cooperation did the impossible, and on Saturday, June 8, 1929, the First Evensong of Sunday was held in the Chapel. It was the first service in this new house of worship. As Sister Beatrice describes it:

> The first chords of the wonderful new organ pealed forth 'Praise God from Whom all blessings flow,' and we sang with lusty and partly husky voice, but from the bottom of our hearts.... We were all thrilled!

The new Chapel was filled with Sisters, children, and the many guests who were arriving for the upcoming consecration celebrations.

During the next two days, chaos reigned again as workmen worked overtime to complete and polish the floors and arrange the furnishings. By late Monday, the altar was prepared and white lilies filled the niches of the reredos. The Community throbbed with excitement and expectancy as visiting bishops and clergy arrived and letters and telegrams of congratulations poured in. The great day was at hand!

The Feast of Saint Barnabas, June 11, 1929, dawned clear and mild. The Sisters had an early Eucharist in the Convent chapel, which now would be referred to as the oratory. At 10 o'clock, Bishop Paul Matthews led Morning Prayer in the new Chapel. He then headed up a small procession into Saint Francis Chapel to unveil the first stained glass window, which depicts the "Canticle of the Sun" of Saint Francis.

Fig. 1.14
Bethany Home Children
Peek through Pew Parapet (c. 1929)

Meanwhile, guests had begun arriving for the public Service of Consecration at 11 A.M., and the Glendale marshal and four assistants were directing traffic along the village streets. The children formed lines in front of their cottages, and the Sisters in front of the Convent.

Eight bishops, almost thirty clergy, and the servers vested in the two sacristies, Saint Francis Chapel, and the undercroft. They all came out in procession through the south door. Sister Beatrice says: "They were all resplendent in vestments, cloth-of-gold copes, mitres and hoods of gorgeous colors.... We surely did things right and brilliantly for once in our lives!"

After the ritual three knocks on the great oak doors by Bishop Paul Matthews, the consecrating bishop, the long procession entered the Chapel, accompanied by the chanting of Psalm 24 (see fig. 1.15). According to Sister Beatrice:

> ...the procession entered babies first, as always in Bethany Home, but the little ones did not stay, they kept right on processing out of the side door, and for the first part of our three-hour service stayed on the lawn until after the grand procession around the Chapel... when they slipped back into the Chapel through a side door and stood in the Crossing in front of the pews, all of which they did very inconspicuously and yet had a very real part in the service and memories for the rest of their lives.

After the opening Psalm, Bishop Matthews took his seat and the contractor, Frank Hamer, came forward. He read his testimony that he was the master builder and that he certified the Chapel was well and conscientiously built. Then he delivered a large, wooden key to the bishop to symbolize the turning over of the responsibility for the building to the consecrator. James Cleveland, as trustee of the Society of the Transfiguration, read the "Instrument of Donation," certifying that the building was free from debt.

The Service of Consecration proceeded with smaller processions to the font, the rood screen, the altar rail, the high altar, and other locations for blessings, dedicating them to the glory of God. The procession was accompanied by the singing of hymns. The "Sentence of Consecration" was then read. Next, the marble mason, Otto Kadon, knelt in his overalls and chiseled a small Maltese cross in the marble step in front of the altar as a seal of consecration. Sister Beatrice remembers: "Bishop Matthews stood just in front at the altar watching him, making a most beautiful picture robed in cloth of gold and wearing a most gorgeous miter."

Then followed a grand procession of bishops, clergy, and Sisters around the entire Chapel, while the children sang hymns they had practiced all year long under the direction of church musician and carillonneur John Prower Symons. The Service concluded with the Eucharist, celebrated by Bishop Sheldon M. Griswold, with Bishop Irving Johnson as preacher.

Immediately after the Service, the bishops signed the hand-illuminated document, "Sentence of Consecration," each attaching his seal and initializing it.

Following the Service, there was a festive lunch on the lawn, prepared and served by Associates and Bethany Home girls. Then, at three in the afternoon, Bishop Matthews confirmed ten Bethany Home girls and the mother of two of them.

Fig. 1.15
Children in Procession

Fig. 1.16
Interment of the Body
of Mother Eva Mary

The day concluded on a solemn note, with the arrival of the body of Mother Eva Mary from its vault at Spring Grove Cemetery. In Sister Beatrice's words:

> We had the altar removed to one side of the Chancel and the body of our dearest Mother came home to us about five o'clock and was placed over the open vault and covered with the very beautiful blue and white pall, and the large floral cross from Bishop Matthews and wreath from Mrs. Gray were placed upon it. Then the temporary Altar was put in place. It was made especially and covered the casket as a large table. Vigil started at once and was kept up all night, three Sisters to a vigil of two hours length.

The Burial of the Reverend Mother Eva Mary

It was fitting that the entombment of the Community's foundress was the first major service to be held in the new Chapel after its consecration (see fig. 1.16). Mother Eva had died July 6, 1928, just as the Chapel that she and Sister Beatrice envisioned from the earliest days of the Community was beginning to take shape. Sister Beatrice describes the entombment:

> The Requiem was at seven-thirty the next day. Bishop Matthews had preached a wonderful sermon at the Consecration service, he also celebrated the Mass at the Requiem.... At this service the front seats in the choir were filled with Mother's near relatives.... The admission to this service was by special invitation as we only wanted her near and dear friends present but the Church was crowded with children, Associates and friends. Sister Ruth was organist for this service and we sang Cobb's Mass. Our Altar rail holds eighteen and there were a great many communions made that morning. After the Requiem the temporary Altar was carried out of the Church, down into the Chapter Room where from henceforth it will be our Chapter Room table. Then Bishop Matthews had the Committal Service, and all of the Sisters and relatives who were sitting in the Choir drew close to the open vault, as before an open grave, while the body was lowered. The casket had been resting on a lowering device over the open vault and at the proper moment the undertaker came up and almost by magic the casket descended, slowly and irrevocably out of sight. The new flowers as well as the faded flowers she carried twenty-six years ago at her service of Profession were placed in the vault with her. Then the service closed and again we left the Chapel quietly without any particular procession. A hot breakfast was served in the Children's Refectory by those dear, faithful Associates. The cover to the grave vault was put in place and sealed immediately, then the temporary floor was put back, the big altar was replaced in preparation for the first service of the Associates Retreat which began at three o'clock that afternoon.

During the committal, a beautifully symbolic gesture occurred when several of the bishops, including Mother Eva's own brother, Bishop Matthews, made the sign of the cross on the head of the casket with mingled dust from Glendale, Ohio and Mount Tabor in Palestine, believed by many to be the site of the Transfiguration of Our Lord.

Sister Beatrice wrote later in *The Living Church* that Mother Eva's Requiem was a glorious thanksgiving for her life and work. "As we entered the Chapel in the early morning, her finished material works lay spread out before us. The lovely children's village (Bethany) clustered about the Chapel as a center.... and [now] the Chapel itself..." It was, she said, "a celebration by the Community of the completion of the life work of the Mother Foundress, Mother Eva Mary..." (Notable 1929, 330)

Other Special Events in the Chapel

The building has been hallowed through the years by worship, prayers, and services without number: Eucharist, Morning Prayer, Evensong, Baptism, Confirmation, weddings, funerals, and many others.

Since June, 1929, all milestones in the life of the Community have taken place in the Chapel. This includes the reception of postulants into the Community, the clothing of novices, and the Sisters' profession of vows. The installation of Mother Superiors always has taken place in the Chapel as well.

Following Mother Eva and Sister Beatrice, the Mother Superiors and their terms have been Sister Clara Elizabeth (1938–43), Sister Olivia Mary (1943–53), Sister Louise Magdalene (1953–63 and 1973–1983), Sister Esther Mary (1963–1973), Sister Ann Margaret (1983–1993 and 1998–2003), and Sister Alice Lorraine (1993–1998) (see figs. 1.17, 1.18).

Since the Chapel was built, the Sisters' life professions have been held here – beautiful, solemn, joyful occasions all. The first was that of Sister Marion Beatrice and Sister Rose Marie on June 18, 1931, followed shortly by that of Sister Dorothea Mary on October 4, 1931.

The picturesque, intimate beauty of the Chapel has made it a favorite site for weddings over the years. The first wedding in the Chapel was that of Fritz Abplanalp, the Chapel's master woodcarver, and Elisabeth Mader on January 14, 1931. The service was conducted in both German and English, since Elisabeth had just arrived from Switzerland and did not speak English. Since then, former Bethany students, their children, and now their grandchildren have celebrated their weddings in the Chapel of the Transfiguration. Numerous Associates, relatives, and friends of the Sisters have chosen the Chapel as their wedding place, too.

> *"May God grant a continual flow of His grace to all who seek it earnestly in this Chapel in the years to come."*
>
> – Sister Beatrice

Fig. 1.17
Mother Superiors from 1928 through 1953
(l. to r.) Sisters Olivia Mary (niece of Mother Eva Mary), Louise Magdalene, Clara Elizabeth, and Beatrice Martha

Fig. 1.18
Mother Superiors from 1953 to Present
(l. to r.) Sisters Esther Mary, Ann Margaret, Alice Lorraine, and Louise Magdalene

Fig. 1.19
A Wedding in the Chapel of
the Transfiguration

Fig. 1.20
Infant Baptism

Fig. 1.21
Birthday Blessings for Bethany
School Students

During the 1930s, the return of Sisters from Hawaii or China via ocean liner and train was among the most thrilling events for Sisters and children alike. If the hour was suitable, Sisters and children met the traveling Sisters at the Glendale railroad station and escorted them in procession to the Chapel. There the bells were rung and the "Te Deum" was sung, rising to the massive Douglas fir rafters!

The Chapel has been the place of worship and celebration for three important occasions, which took place twenty-five years apart.

- On August 6, 1948, the Community celebrated the fiftieth anniversary of its founding. At that time, the first of the stained glass windows in the nave were dedicated;

- On March 4, 1973, the last Sunday of Epiphany, the Community celebrated its seventy-fifth anniversary. The new church lectionary had designated that Sunday as an observance of the Transfiguration, so in effect the Community now had two patronal festivals: the last Sunday in Epiphany and August 6. This date was chosen because the hot, humid Cincinnati summers make the non-air conditioned Chapel an uncomfortable place for a large crowd;

- On February 22, 1998, again the last Sunday of Epiphany, the Community celebrated its hundredth anniversary. This time the weather was not the only reason for selecting the alternate date. In August, all bishops in the Anglican Communion would be assembled in England for the Lambeth Conference, which takes place every ten years. The preacher for the hundredth anniversary was the newly installed Presiding Bishop of the Episcopal Church, The Right Reverend Frank Griswold. He replaced the Right Reverend John M. Allin, former Presiding Bishop and chaplain general of the Community, who could not come because of illness.

Each of these celebrations was a glorious affair, attended by members of other religious communities and clergy from all over the United States, Canada, and Great Britain, as well as many other guests. The fruitfulness and influence of the work begun by Mother Eva was aptly noted by the Right Reverend Paul Matthews during his sermon at the fiftieth anniversary: "Here she dug a well, as in the desert, and behold a fertile field."

Over the years, the Chapel of the Transfiguration has hosted concerts, conferences and retreats, Bethany School assembles, graduations, baptisms, pageants, and weddings (see figs. 1.19-1.21). It is a place where sins have been confessed, petitions have been made, thanksgivings and praises have been raised to God, and miracles have happened. Meditations and prayers of many different people from all over the world have been offered here – all in an atmosphere of peace and joy.

✠

100TH ANNIVERSARY CELEBRATIONS

Community of the Transfiguration
1898-1998

CHAPEL OF THE TRANSFIGURATION

I was glad when they said to me,

"Let us go to the house of the Lord."

(Psalm 122:1)

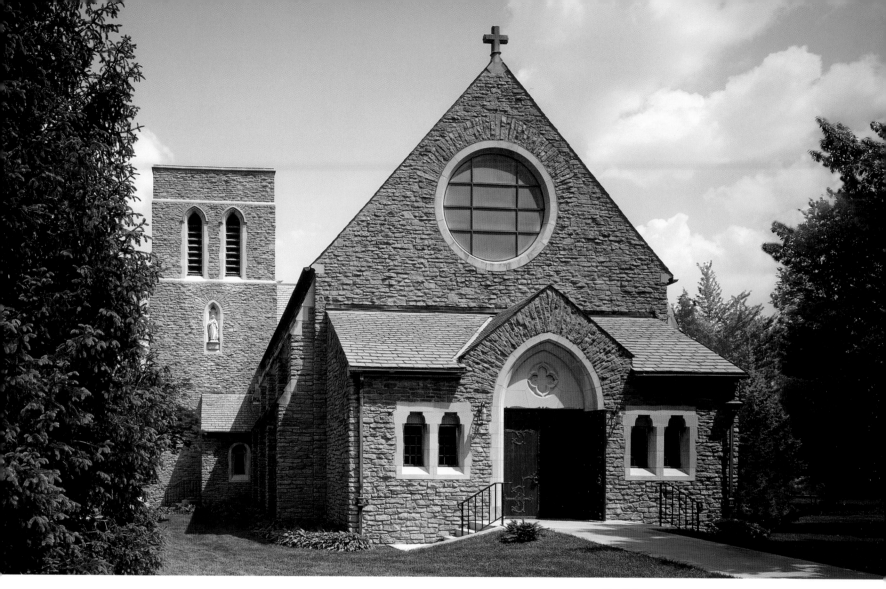

Fig. 2.1
Chapel of the Transfiguration (exterior view)
Latin cross at peak 36 in. (height)
24 in. (across) (approx.)

nter the gates of the Community of the Transfiguration, and prepare to be welcomed by delightful flower gardens, gracious trees, and the unmistakable sense of quiet and peace that surrounds an unforgettable treasure: the Chapel of the Transfiguration.

No matter what the season of the year, the Chapel stands as a beautiful, much-loved limestone gem set into Community grounds, located in the quiet suburban village of Glendale, Ohio. Architecturally, it is the centerpiece of the compound that comprises what was, in the late 1890s, Bethany Home and the Convent of the Transfiguration. Today, as over one hundred years ago, the air is often vibrant with the voices of children, as well as those of the Sisters, Associates, residents, and guests.

Mother Foundress Eva Mary originally envisioned Bethany Home for children as an English village with cottages and school surrounding the church. In keeping with Mother Eva's plans, the Chapel is of English Village, neo-Gothic style (see fig. 2.1). It is constructed of local, water-worn limestone brought from the Little Miami River near Loveland, Ohio.

Fig. 2.2
Statue of Good Shepherd in Bell Tower
48 in. (height)

Fig. 2.3
Main Entrance of Chapel (west end)
tracery with quatrefoil 32 in. dia.
door 36 in. x 94 in. x 3 in. (each)

A close examination of the Chapel's sedimentary river stone exterior reveals a fascinating myriad of fossils typical of those found in Southern Ohio stream beds, including brachiopods, trilobites, and cephalopods. Indiana also made a natural contribution to the Chapel construction. The trimming stones used around the doors and windows are, according to the architect's specifications, "…buff Indiana limestone, of the best quality and free from all defects." (*Specifications* 1927, 34)

The roof is covered with "Vermont unfading green slates, acceptable to the architects…. All to be full quarter-inch in thickness, nailed securely with two nails to each slate." (*Specifications* 1927, 36) A glance upward to the apex of the roof's west end reveals a simple Latin cross; below, a round stained glass window. Above the door, in a simple Gothic plate tracery, is a quatrefoil (see fig. 2.3).

The Chapel bell tower houses a carillon of thirty-six bells, descendant of the original carillon installed in 1931, and a clavier. It is also home to a statue of the Good Shepherd, holding a lamb against His left shoulder while the sheep at His feet looks up at Him. Now tucked high in a niche on the outside west wall of the bell tower, the statue was once in residence at the former Convent on the grounds. For many years, the statue had provided an opportunity for children to pet the lamb as they passed. Remarkably, the bell tower niche was designed before it was realized that the statue would fit perfectly (see fig. 2.2). The Chapel cornerstone is located in the northeast corner of the bell tower.

English ivy grows up the walls of the Chapel and on the ground nearby. It was started from a slip that Sister Beatrice brought back from the Hermitage at Ascot Priory, a convalescent home for the indigent sick in London established by Mother Priscilla Lydia Sellon near Ascot, England in 1861. At that time, it was in the country, west of London. One of the stained glass windows in the Chapel honors this religious pioneer.

The Sisters call this ivy the "Pusey Ivy" in honor of Dr. Edward Bouverie Pusey, a foremost leader in the revival of religious and liturgical life in the Anglican Communion during the nineteenth century. Dr. Pusey and many others turned to the Hermitage at Ascot Priory as a place of physical and spiritual refreshment. It was to Ascot Priory that he retired, and he died there in 1882 (Anson 1955, 277).

A flagstone-edged sidewalk leads to the main entrance of the Chapel of the Transfiguration, with its impressive double doors of solid white oak, hung with enormous, elaborately tooled brass hinges (see fig. 2.3). When these west-facing doors are opened, this doorway is aligned through the narthex, the nave, and the choir to the altar at the east end, representing "the straight and narrow path that leads to salvation." (Matt. 7: 13-14)

The Chapel entryway, or narthex, takes its name from the Greek and is derived from a Sanskrit root meaning "reed." This usually long, narrow room is suggestive of the hollow stem of the plant. In early Christianity, such an area was placed at the west end of a church to accommodate penitents and catechumens, who were preparing to be baptized and received into the Church (Whone 1977, 117).

The narthex of the Chapel of the Transfiguration serves not only as an entryway, but also, for practical purposes, as a cloakroom. Eight feet wide by twenty-six feet long, it is sparsely furnished with a few benches.

On the south wall of the narthex hangs a hand-illuminated copy of the Sentence of Consecration, dated June 11, 1929 and attested to by the bishops participating in that historic occasion: Boyd Vincent of Southern Ohio, Sheldon M. Griswold of Chicago, Albion W. Knight of New Jersey, James Wise of Kansas, Irving P. Johnson of Colorado, Thomas Jenkins of Nevada, and Paul Matthews of New Jersey. Their diocesan seals appear on the document (see fig. 2.4).

Another wall displays a photograph of a mosaic of stones that is located in the footpace, or priest's step, in front of the altar, along with a key to their origins (see fig. 2.5). In 1907, Mother

Fig. 2.5
Photograph of Stone Mosaic
14 in. x 14½ in. (with frame)

Fig. 2.4
Sentence of Consecration
20 in. x 29 in. (with frame)

Eva and Sister Beatrice visited religious communities and places of pilgrimage in the British Isles. They brought back these stones from holy places such as Iona, Lindisfarne, and Canterbury with the dream that someday the stones would be placed in a Convent chapel. Sister Beatrice later wrote: "It became a habit of mine to pick up a stone as we went to the holy places, later to be made into a pavement in front of the high altar… symbolic that the priests serving at our altar are standing on an Anglican foundation." (Beatrice 1940, 105)

A third wall holds two lists of the honor members of Saint Mary's Altar Guild, which had its beginning at Bethany Home and which has evolved over the years to become a Servers Guild. Names of girls who had done outstanding work are included on the lists, which reflect the years from 1936 to 1973.

In the early days of Bethany Home, Mother Eva formed Saint Mary's Guild as a devotional group for confirmed girls. Members followed a simple rule of life and met once a week with Mother Eva for spiritual instructions. The Guild later became an altar guild, which combined the devotional life with practical training in altar work (see figs. 2.6, 2.7).

In 1977, when Bethany School no longer had boarding students, the guild was disbanded. The following year, a Servers Guild was established to include both boys and girls. To this day, the Servers Guild continues to do altar guild work for Bethany School worship services, which are held in the Chapel.

> *"It became a habit of mine to pick up a stone as we went to the holy places…"*
>
> – Sister Beatrice

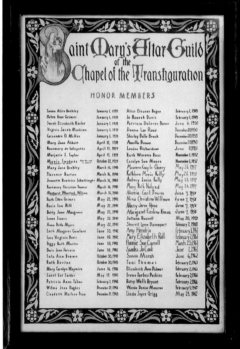

Fig. 2.6
Honor Members of St. Mary's Altar Guild
first list
20 in. x 28 in. (with frame)

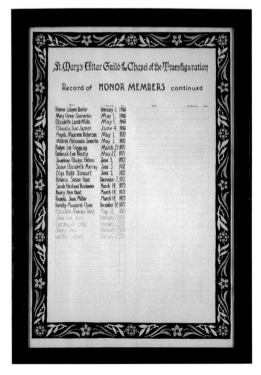

Fig. 2.7
Honor Members of St. Mary's Altar Guild
second list
20 in x 28 in. (with frame)

Elegant woodcarvings – on the pews, walls, and throughout the Chapel – first catch the eye of visitors to the Chapel of the Transfiguration. Then, no sooner do visitors delight at the wonderful woodworkings, than they begin to notice the Renaissance paintings and artwork, and then quietly appreciate the warm, beautiful wooden cathedral ceiling and rafters of the nave (see fig. 2.8).

The nave is the main body of a church building where the congregation is seated and participates in the various forms of liturgy. The word nave comes from the Latin "navis," meaning ship. It is so called because the massively beamed ceilings of churches and cathedrals resemble the shape of an inverted ship. In sacred symbolism, the Church is like Noah's ark: with its Word and Sacraments, it reflects the sacred vessel that carries humanity through the storms of life and time.

The cathedral ceiling and rafters of the Chapel's nave are of Douglas fir from Mount Shasta, California. They were fabricated by Irving Casson and Company, Boston, Massachusetts. The floors are double. The lower floor is of North Carolina yellow pine, overlaid with a finishing floor of kiln dried plain white oak.

The beauty and quality of the woodwork make the Chapel a unique example of neo-Gothic architecture. Woodcarvings throughout the Chapel are largely the work of two Swiss carvers: Sister Clara Elizabeth (1873-1958) (see fig. 2.9) and Fritz Abplanalp (1907-1977) (see fig. 2.10).

Sister Clara arrived in Glendale, Ohio in 1907 with a strong sense of vocation to the Community of the

Fig. 2.8
Nave of Chapel

Fig. 2.9
Sister Clara Elizabeth (1873-1958)
woodcarver; Mother Superior
(1938-43)

Fig. 2.10
Fritz Abplanalp (1907-1977)
Swiss woodcarver

Fig. 2.11
Motifs for Chapel Carvings
Wheat and Grapes (left)
Panel with Medallion (center)
Angel Head (right)

Transfiguration. She was life professed in 1910, and later served as Superior of the Community from 1938 to 1943. In her native Switzerland, this young woman had been a woodcarving teacher, and the Community immediately recognized her talent. Not long after Sister Clara's arrival, the tiny oratory in the former Convent, later destroyed by fire, was made more beautiful and rich with her carving.

On a visit to Switzerland while the Chapel was under construction, Sister Clara selected a young Swiss woodcarver, Fritz Abplanalp, for employment by the Community. He arrived in April, 1929, just two months before the Chapel's consecration, and began his carvings for the Chapel under the architects' and Sister Clara's supervision.

The reredos, rood screen, and altar rail were already in place when Fritz arrived, having been crafted by two American firms: Irving Casson and Company and Robert Mitchell Manufacturing Company. They had followed closely the architects' clear specifications for these items:

> All carving shall be executed by skilled workmen of such firms as are approved by the architects. It may be roughed out by machine, but the entire surface must be re-cut and finished by hand, the carver continuously varying slightly the design in such manner as may be directed or approved by the architects. The contractor is to furnish models of all carving and to submit them to the architects for approval before commencing work (*Specifications* 1926, 53).

The carvings are of very high quality. The reredos and altar became sources of unifying themes for Fritz. He used the wheat and grapes design from the border of the reredos, along with the angel head and panel with a small medallion from its lower corners (see fig. 2.11). From the altar he used the frieze carvings in the retables and the monk and nun figures on the front edge of the ends of the altar.

Fritz's prolific, well-executed work includes the Stations of the Cross, the first pew parapet, and the last pew ends in the nave. His art also includes virtually all the rich and extensive carvings in the choir and sanctuary: the figures of the apostles and their angels on the rood screen, ambo, choir stalls and canopy, misericords and medallions, altar rail, angel statues in the reredos, credence table, and four prie-dieus with chairs. He also carved the crucifix used during Holy Week and the Good Shepherd statue in Saint Francis Chapel.

All this work Fritz accomplished in less than six years. On a visit many years later, he looked around the Chapel and asked: "Did I do all this?"

During this time, when the young woodcarver was hard at work, his fiancée, Elisabeth Mader, arrived from Switzerland, and they were married in the Chapel.

As Fritz's work began to near completion, Sister Clara found a woodcarving teaching position for him in Honolulu. He and his wife, with their two children, left for Hawaii in 1935. Five of the fourteen Stations of the Cross remained to be completed.

Eventually, Fritz retired in California and made frequent trips home to Switzerland, often stopping at the Convent en route. On one of those trips, Fritz was asked whether he might finish the Stations. The master Swiss woodcarver declined, saying that his style had changed and that he felt he could not complete them in the same spirit.

In the late 1980s, the Stations that Fritz had completed were removed from storage in the Chapel undercroft, cleaned, and hung in their present location on the north, west, and south walls of the nave, together with the five plaster casts of Stations-in-progress. The plaster models remain as evidence of his exacting work process. For each of the Stations, Fritz first shaped the scene in clay, made a mold of it with plaster, then cast a model from the mold in plaster. Finally, he executed the models in wood (see figs. 2.12-2.25).

STATIONS OF THE CROSS

The Stations of the Cross represent Christ's progression from his trial to his death on Calvary. Beginning next to the north door of the nave, the first nine stations in the Chapel of the Transfiguration are walnut carvings. The last five are unfinished plaster models (see figs. 2.12–2.25). All are 15 in. x 20 in.

Fig. 2.12
First Station
Jesus is condemned to death.

Fig. 2.13
Second Station
Jesus takes the cross upon His shoulders.

Fig. 2.14
Third Station
Jesus falls the first time beneath the cross.

Fig 2.15
Fourth Station
Jesus meets His mother.

Fig 2.16
Fifth Station
Simon of Cyrene is compelled to help Jesus carry His cross.

Fig 2.17
Sixth Station
Veronica wipes His face with her napkin.

Fig. 2.18
Seventh Station
Jesus falls the second time beneath the cross.

Fig. 2.19
Eighth Station
Jesus speaks to the wailing women.

Fig. 2.20
Ninth Station
Jesus falls the third time beneath the cross.

Fig. 2.21
Tenth Station
Jesus is stripped of His garments.

Fig. 2.22
Eleventh Station
Jesus is nailed to the cross.

Fig. 2.23
Twelfth Station
Jesus dies on the cross.

Fig. 2.24
Thirteenth Station
Jesus is taken down from the cross.

Fig. 2.25
Fourteenth Station
Jesus is laid in the tomb.

Fig. 2.26
Pew End
21 in. x 36 in. x 3½ in.

Robert Mitchell Manufacturing Company, Cincinnati, Ohio, built the rich, black walnut pews in the nave. Sister Clara, along with some fellow Sisters and older Bethany Home girls, carved most of the pew ends. They began their work in 1924, years before there was even a mark on an architect's drawing. On each pew end, the carving bears a Latin cross or the Jerusalem Cross, which is the symbol of the Community, and every carving has representations of flora and fauna. Otherwise no two designs are alike (see fig. 2.26).

There are two rows of fourteen pews, although Mother Eva and Sister Beatrice planned for only thirteen double rows. When the Chapel was completed, there was room for one more double row of pews in the back of the nave. Fritz Abplanalp carved these four pew ends.

The Chapel was planned to accommodate all members of the Community, from Sisters to students, family members, and visitors. In keeping with that plan, the front pews were designed for very young children. Instead of a solid parapet, Fritz fashioned arches through which the little ones could have a better view of the proceedings. So that short little legs wouldn't dangle, the first row seat is twelve inches from the floor and the second row, fourteen inches (see fig. 2.27).

Fig 2.27
Parapet
96 in. long
Parapet end
11 in. x 36 in. x 3½ in.

NAVE WINDOWS

There is a familiar tale of a child who, asked what a saint is, looked to the stained glass windows and replied, "A saint is one the light shines through." In the nave windows of the Chapel of the Transfiguration, light shines through centuries of devotion and sainthood.

Sister Beatrice suggested the subject matter for the lancet windows in the nave. In a departure from the tradition of having such windows portray biblical scenes and events, she suggested that they should show personages significant in the history and development of religious life, particularly in the Anglican Communion. In keeping with her suggestion, the Chapel's nave windows introduce us to God's luminous saints, who rooted English religious life in the third and fourth century Celtic tradition, and to those leaders who courageously recovered the traditions of religious life in the nineteenth and early twentieth centuries, both in England and in North America. The round window in the west wall reflects the devotion of the Community to the care of children.

At the time of its consecration, the Chapel had only one stained glass window: the "Canticle of the Sun" window, located in Saint Francis Chapel. Other windows were of amber glass, examples of which can still be seen in the windows in the narthex and in the chapter room in the Chapel undercroft.

It was quickly evident that the large round window in the west wall allowed a strong glare during Evensong, and the Sisters looked forward to replacing it with stained glass. This would, however, have to wait until funds could be raised.

The process began in 1946. Sister Beatrice was appointed co-chairperson of the planning committee, along with Sister Anna Grace. Sister Constance Anna, an enthusiastic and creative fundraiser, was appointed treasurer and went immediately into action. The hope was to have the first windows installed in time for the Community's fiftieth anniversary. That goal was met. The round window and three lancet windows were installed in time for the celebration on August 6, 1948. The process of beautifying the Chapel through stained glass continued until the final window, the Saint Clare window in Saint Francis Chapel, was installed in 1960.

Two firms were responsible for the Chapel windows. Charles J. Connick Studios, Boston, Massachusetts produced all of the windows except those in the sanctuary, and Riordan Stained Glass Studio, a Cincinnati, Ohio firm since 1838, produced the five sanctuary windows. The work was done under the direction of Dr. Ralph Adams Cram and his architectural firm in Boston, who contracted for the construction of the Chapel.

The lancet windows in the north wall portray pre-Reformation abbesses or founders of religious orders. The lancet windows in the south wall show founders of Anglican religious communities since their revival in the Church of England in 1845.

"A saint is one
the light shines through"

Windows on the North Side of the Nave

Saint Boniface
Saint Lioba

The windows of Saints Boniface and Lioba commemorate two early trailblazing religious leaders. They were bound together not only as kin, but also by their fervent missionary work in Germany.

SAINT BONIFACE

As you enter the nave from the north side door, the first window nearest the rood screen is that of Saint Boniface (680-754). Born in England, he became a monk and later a priest, bishop, and archbishop. Inspired by the examples of Willibrord and other Christian missionaries, Boniface was commissioned by Pope Gregory II for missionary work in Germany, where he established churches and monasteries in Hesse, Thuringia, and Bavaria. Although his work received support from many of the Frankish rulers, Boniface's teaching and actions brought him into conflict with dedicated followers of the ancient pagan religions. While waiting to confirm a group of converts on June 5, 754, he and his companions were attacked and murdered by a group of pagans. He was buried at Fulda, a monastery he founded near Mainz, Germany (*Proper* 1998, 250).

In the lancet window, Saint Boniface is shown vested with cope and miter and carrying a crozier (see figs. 2.28, 2.29). Above is the martyr's crown, and below is a Bible, pierced by a sword to indicate the manner of his death. Boniface had ordered his

Fig. 2.28
Lancet Windows
north wall, east end

Saint Boniface (r.)
dedicated October 18, 1948
Feast of Saint Luke
20 in. x 110 in.

Saint Lioba (l.)
dedicated May 10, 1959
20 in. x 110 in.

followers not to fight the pagans who were attacking him and, laying his head on the Bible, received his death blow. The principal medallion in the window reflects the occasion when Boniface chopped down an oak tree, sacred to the devotees of pagan religion, in order to demonstrate the powerlessness of the local gods. Near the tree is a suggestion of the church he built using the wood of the fallen tree. At the base of the window is the symbol of Saint Lioba, kinswoman to Saint Boniface and a dearly loved companion in service to Christ and in the building up of the religious life. The window text: "They that turn many to righteousness shall shine as the stars forever and ever" (Dan. 12:3).

Saint Lioba

The companion window to Saint Boniface shows Saint Lioba (c. 700-780). In the first half of the eighth century, Anglo-Saxon monasticism – particularly Benedictine – was instrumental in spreading Christian faith, practice, and scholarship throughout Northern Europe. Many women were actively involved in this missionary effort and accepted as educators and administrators equally with men.

One of these women was a West Saxon nun, Thrutgeba, known in England as "Leofe" ("the dear one") and in Germany as "Lioba" ("beloved"). Lioba's mother was a relative of Boniface. At the age of twenty-one, Lioba made her profession of vows at Wimborne Abbey in England, where she had been placed as a child. Hearing of Boniface's work in Germany, the young nun wrote to him, asking prayers and counsel. As a result, when he was organizing several convents, Boniface requested that Lioba and several other nuns be sent to Germany to plant the seed there. Lioba went, along with her cousin Thecla and about thirty others. Lioba was put in charge of the monastery called Bischofsheim (Bishop's Home) in Mainz, Germany, which flourished under her care. From Bischofsheim, nuns founded houses in other parts of Germany (Thurston 1956, 3:668).

A wise abbess, Lioba lived simply and abstemiously, and refused to permit spiritual excesses. This sensible life gave her the energy for pastoral care of her nuns, oversight of the many businesses of the Convent, the extensive study and teaching in which she delighted, and active engagement in the life of prayer and worship (Thurston 1956, 3:668). The work of Lioba and other women in worship, education, good works, spiritual growth, healing, and communal life sets a high standard for those in religious life today.

This lancet window commemorates both Saint Lioba and the work of the Community of the Transfiguration in China. The first overseas mission of the Community was called Saint Lioba's Compound. Located in Wuhu, China, it was established at the request of Bishop Daniel T. Huntington of Anking, China. The window image shows Saint Lioba wearing a crown and holding an abbess's crozier and a flask of holy oil on top of a closed book (see figs. 2.28, 2.30). Above is a symbol of Saint Lioba's Compound. Below are two Chinese Sisters carrying a patient on a stretcher to Stanley Memorial Building in the Compound. The principal medallion portrays two Sisters of the Transfiguration preaching the Gospel to a group of Chinese people. The final medallion presents a Chinese Sister teaching school children. The window text: "Let the word of Christ dwell in you richly" (Col. 3:16).

Fig. 2.29
Saint Boniface Window
principal medallion – detail
Boniface cuts down an oak tree.

Fig. 2.30
Saint Lioba Window
principal medallion – detail
Sisters preach the Gospel.

Saint Bride (Brigid)
Saint Hilda

The next set of lancet windows portrays two strong women leaders of great influence, both saints of the early Celtic Church and abbesses of double monasteries of men and women. Both were advisors to the church and to political leaders.

Saint Bride (Brigid)

Saint Brigid (453-523) is identified in the lancet window as St. Bride, the name by which she is known in England and Scotland. One of the most beloved saints of Ireland, she is believed to have been the daughter of Dubhthach, a druid and court poet to King Loeghaire, the High King. Her mother was a slave in the king's household. At an early age, Brigid was converted to Christianity and, while a young woman, dedicated her life to Christ as a nun. She was renowned for her extraordinary generosity and compassion for those in need, and many of the miracles attributed to her involve meeting the needs of the poor.

In 470, Brigid founded a convent at Kildare, a town whose name means "The Church of the Oak," with a group of women. A community of monks joined them later, thus forming the only double monastery known in Ireland. Under Brigid's leadership, the monastery became the See of the province.

Brigid participated in several of the ecumenical councils of Ireland and was influential in shaping Irish political life. Well-known as a "soul friend" or spiritual director of many priests and bishops, she is a popular saint across the British Isles. In Wales, she is known as Ffraid (Clarke 1968, 1; *Proper* 1998, 136).

Fig. 2.31
Lancet Windows
north wall, center
dedicated March 25, 1949
Feast of the Annunciation

Saint Bride (r.)
20 in. x 110 in.

Saint Hilda (l.)
20 in. x 110 in.

In the lancet window honoring her, Saint Brigid is shown with the abbess's crozier and a bowl of milk (see figs. 2.31, 2.32). Above her is a symbol of the perpetual fire, which the convent at Kildare kept burning on the site of an ancient druid fire. Below is a cow, representing her generous gifts of butter and milk to the poor. The principal medallion represents the legend of Saint Brigid's healing of a leper. The woman is holding the bell carried by lepers to warn others of the danger of contagion. Saint Brigid offers her a bowl of water that, legend claims, turned into a bowl of healing milk. The final medallion portrays the oak tree near her cell. The window text: "I found Him whom my soul loveth" (Song of Sol. 3:4).

SAINT HILDA

The companion window honors Saint Hilda (614-680), daughter of Hereric, nephew of King Edwin of Northumbria. Hilda was baptized at the age of thirteen, along with King Edwin. Her Aunt Ethelburga, the queen, nurtured her in the faith. (Ethelburga is the subject of another lancet window in the Chapel.)

Fig. 2.32
Saint Bride Window
principal medallion – detail
Brigid heals a leper.

After twenty years in the court of King Edwin, Hilda decided to enter the monastic life. With the help of Aidan, Bishop of Lindisfarne, Hilda founded religious houses for both men and women. Her foundation at Whitby, in Yorkshire, was a center of scholarship and creativity, where both nuns and monks lived in obedience to Hilda's rule of justice, devotion, chastity, peace, and charity. A woman of commanding appearance and noble character, Hilda led the abbey for two decades as administrator, teacher, and spiritual guide.

Hilda's greatness emerges, in part, through the lives of those she taught and influenced and through her church leadership. Five monks from Whitby Abbey became bishops. Hilda also taught and encouraged the famous unlettered poet Caedmon, who composed songs about Biblical stories. She served as translator and advisor at the Council of Whitby, convened in 663 at Whitby Abbey to resolve the divisive questions regarding traditions of Celtic Christians and followers of the Roman order. Hilda and her community favored the Celtic position, but when the Roman position prevailed, they reluctantly accepted it in an act of painful obedience (Clarke 1968, 297; *Proper* 1998, 400).

The window portraying Hilda shows her with the abbess's crozier and an open book (see figs. 2.31, 2.33). Above is a suggestion of Whitby Abbey, and below a medallion showing three serpents. These symbolize the legend that she eradicated a serpent infestation from the Abbey. The principal medallion shows Hilda receiving the veil from Bishop Aidan. The last medallion presents a wild goose, the Celtic symbol of the Holy Spirit. The window text: "She openeth her mouth with wisdom" (Prov. 31:26).

Fig. 2.33
Saint Hilda Window
principal medallion – detail
Hilda receives the veil.

Saint Ethelburga
Saint Frideswide

The final pair of windows on the north wall depicts two great Anglo-Saxon foundresses: Saint Ethelburga (d.c.647) and Saint Frideswide (d.c.735). Both were of royal birth and women of significant influence.

SAINT ETHELBURGA

Saint Ethelburga was a daughter of Bertha and Ethelbert, the first Christian king of Kent and the founder of the See of Canterbury. From her mother, who established the first place of Christian worship at Canterbury, Ethelburga learned to draw close to God. Sent to Northumbria to marry King Edwin, she was instrumental in converting him and many members of his family to Christianity. On Easter Eve, 627, the king was baptized in a wooden church on the future site of York Cathedral at the same time as Saint Hilda (also portrayed in a Chapel lancet window). After this event, thousands of people in Northumbria accepted Christianity. Ethelburga returned to Kent following Edwin's death and founded the Convent of Lyming, where she eventually became abbess (Thurston 1956, 2:35).

Saint Ethelburga is shown wearing the queen's crown and holding the abbess's crozier (see figs. 2.34, 2.35). Above is a star, recalling the saying: "She shone as a star in a heathen court." Below, shells suggest the many converts that she baptized. The principal medallion shows Ethelburga holding a trowel and laying the cornerstone of the convent she founded at Lyming. At the base, an angel with a cross symbolizes another saying: "She went as an obedient angel to plant the blessed rood." The window text: "Be thou faithful . . . and I will give thee a crown of life" (Rev. 2:10).

Fig. 2.34
Lancet Windows, north wall, west end
dedicated December, 1957

Saint Ethelburga (r.)
20 in. x 110 in.

Saint Frideswide (l.)
20 in. x 110 in.

Saint Frideswide

Saint Frideswide, patron saint of Oxford, was the daughter of the King of Lower Mercia, Didan, and his wife Sefrida. Born at her father's palace in Oxford, she was raised by a governess who greatly influenced the young princess, teaching her that "whatever is not God is nothing." From an early age, Frideswide inclined towards the religious life. She was very beautiful, a fact that attracted the attention of Aelfgar, the Earl of Leicester, who wanted to marry her. Frideswide refused him, as she had decided that her call was to religious life, but he persisted and invaded Oxford with an army in hope of capturing her. According to legend, Aelfgar was blinded, and his sight restored as a result of her prayers of intercession. Frideswide and two companion nuns fled in a sailboat. Again according to legend, the boat was moved by an angel, who looked like a man dressed in white. They took refuge in Abingdon Woods where, the story continues, a fountain sprang up in response to Frideswide's prayers. They returned to Oxford, where she is said to have met a leper who pleaded for a kiss. In the name of Jesus Christ, she kissed the leper, who was healed instantly. Frideswide founded a convent in Oxford where she and her fellow nuns worked for the poor – teaching, nursing, and relieving their miseries. She is buried in Christ Church Cathedral, Oxford (Clarke 1968, 280).

The lancet window portrays Saint Frideswide holding the abbess's crozier and an open book (see figs. 2.34, 2.36). Above her right shoulder is an ox crossing a ford, symbolizing the Oxford convent and her place of birth and burial. Above is a fountain and below is a sailboat with two nuns and an angel. The principal medallion shows Frideswide praying for the restoration of Aelfgar's sight by Jesus' healing touch. Jesus is portrayed in the upper part of the medallion, with His arm pointed to Aelfgar. In the last medallion, she is shown with the leper, who holds a warning bell. The window text: "Signs and wonders may be done by the name of Jesus" (Acts 4:30).

Windows on the South Side of the Nave

Religious life in England was suppressed during the reign of Henry VIII (1491-1547), beginning in the 1530s. In the centuries following, attempts were made to restore religious life, but they did not last long in what had become a strongly Protestant/anti-Roman Catholic country following the bloody reign of Mary Tudor.

The Oxford Movement, which began in 1833, worked to reform the liturgy and worship of the Church of England and to respond with compassion and hard work to the many deep needs of the poor and marginalized. It inspired many women who longed to serve Christ in ways that the rigid religious and social system of Victorian England would not readily permit.

The windows on the south side of the nave commemorate some of the heroic pioneers who heard and answered the call to religious life stirred by the Oxford Movement. It was a bold and risk-filled step for the early men and women responsible for the revival and for those who followed them on this side of the Atlantic Ocean. They were subject to public and private ridicule. Many of the women were cut off from their families, or their families made attempts to force them to return home (Allchin 1958, 52).

Fig. 2.35
Saint Ethelburga Window
principal medallion – detail
Ethelburga lays a cornerstone.

Fig. 2.36
Saint Frideswide Window
principal medallion – detail
Frideswide prays for healing.

Mother Marian
Mother Lydia

Devotion to service marks the lives of these two religious leaders. Dr. Edward B. Pusey, a religious trailblazer himself, supported and helped enable their work, especially on behalf of needy children, girls, and women.

MOTHER MARIAN (MARIAN REBECCA HUGHES)
Marian Rebecca Hughes (1817-1912), daughter of the Reverend Robert Hughes and his wife Martha, was the first known woman in the Anglican Church to take religious vows since the dissolution of the monasteries under Henry VIII. On Trinity Sunday, 1841 she made her vows in the presence of Dr. Edward B. Pusey, her spiritual director. So seemingly small a step by this woman was a giant leap for the Anglican Church. Because her family needed her help, it was eight years before this pioneer could enter fully into the life she had chosen, but she persevered in prayer, learning, and active service among the poorest and most needy, especially children. She lived her vows to the extent that her circumstances permitted.

Marian Hughes traveled to Normandy, where she visited Roman Catholic convents and studied their rules, lives, and practices. This enabled her to later formulate the rule for her own community, and she gained practical advice from the founders and experienced Sisters whom she visited (Anson 1955, 224).

By 1849, this trailblazer was free finally to fully practice her vocation, and, with the agreement of Bishop Samuel Wilberforce of Oxford, formed a sisterhood called the Society of the Most Holy and Undivided Trinity, the fifth religious community to be established in the Church of England.

Fig. 2.37
Lancet Windows
south wall, west end
dedicated November 5, 1959

Mother Marian (r.)
20 in. x 110 in.

Mother Lydia (l.)
20 in. x 110 in.

At the time, a much-needed form of assistance was to create so-called "penitentiaries" for the rescue and help of women who had fallen into prostitution. Mother Marian found her heart moved by the remark of a girl that "she supposed that unless she became 'a naughty girl,' ladies would do nothing for her" (Anson 1955, 292). Her community's many works of mercy included the establishment of the Oxford Middle-Class Day School for Girls, an educational center for training in domestic duties that also provided opportunities for gainful employment.

As you enter the Chapel from its main doors, the window depicting Mother Marian is the first one on the right. She is shown holding a flaming rose, symbol of her many works of charity (see figs. 2.37, 2.38). Above is a dove, representing the Holy Spirit, and below, a girl at prayer. In the principal medallion, Mother Marian is shown taking her vows before Dr. Pusey. The last medallion is believed to be of Ascot Priory. It became a haven for her, Mother Lydia, Dr. Pusey, and many others. The text on the window describes Mother Marian's sense of commitment, as reflected in the prayer in her journal on the day of her taking vows: "Make me to rejoice in the means of taking the burden of His cross more closely to myself" (Allchin 1958, 59). The window text: "Make me rejoice in taking the burden of this cross."

Fig. 2.38
Mother Marian Window
principal medallion – detail
Mother Marian takes her vows.

MOTHER LYDIA (PRISCILLA LYDIA SELLON)

Dr. Edward B. Pusey referred to Priscilla Lydia Sellon (1821-1876) as "the restorer, after three centuries, of the religious life in the English Church," a description given the foundress of the first community to survive in the Church of England (Allchin 1958, 129). The first actual community, The Park Village Sisterhood, later known as the Sisterhood of the Holy Cross, was established in 1845. It merged with Mother Lydia's Sisterhood of the Most Holy Trinity in 1856.

About to leave England for health reasons in 1848, Priscilla Lydia Sellon changed her plans at the last moment because of a public appeal for work among the destitute in Plymouth and Devonport. Here she was gradually joined by others who, with the help of Dr. Pusey, created a community called the Devonport Sisters of Mercy. They set up schools and orphanages and heroically tended the sick in the cholera epidemic of 1848 (Anson 1955, 261).

The young community sent eight members to aid Florence Nightingale during the Crimean War (1854-1856), where they did hard, self-sacrificing duty under conditions of extreme deprivation (Anson 1955, 268). In 1861, they established a convalescent home near Ascot, England. In 1864, they established a girls' school in Lahaina, in the Hawaiian Islands. This made Mother Lydia's community the first to undertake foreign mission work. Among Mother Lydia's greatest contributions to the revival of religious life in the Church of England was her dual emphasis on organized prayer and devoted service.

In 1867, Mother Lydia responded to a call from Bishop Thomas N. Stanley of Honolulu and Queen Emma of Hawaii to build a school in Honolulu. They established Saint Andrew's Priory, an outstanding school for Hawaiian girls that remains a valued presence in the Islands. The Sisterhood of the Most Holy Trinity administered the school until 1902. From 1918 to 1970, the Community of the Transfiguration assumed responsibility for it (Anson 1955, 278).

Fig. 2.39
Mother Lydia Window
principal medallion – detail
Saint Andrew's Priory
students process.

Mother Lydia's window shows her with the abbess's crozier and holding a model of the chapel of Saint Andrew's Priory School (see figs. 2.37, 2.39). At the top is a broken sword, symbol of the beatitude of the merciful and suggesting the many works of mercy undertaken by the Sisters of the Most Holy Trinity. In the scene below are an ocean steamer and an open boat with

Sisters of the Transfiguration arriving in Honolulu in 1918. The principal medallion shows a procession of Priory girls in their distinctive uniforms of white middy blouses and navy blue skirts. The last medallion portrays the coral cross of Saint Andrew's Priory. The window text, taken from a letter written by Mother Lydia: "Kindle in my heart the fire of divine love."

Mother Harriet Monsell
John Mason Neale

The middle set of windows on the south side of the nave shows, respectively, the first superior of one of the largest religious communities in the Church of England and one of the leaders of the Oxford Movement.

MOTHER HARRIET MONSELL

Devout, dedicated, and hard-working, Mother Harriet Monsell once was described by Dr. John Mason Neale as "one of the most sensible women I ever saw" (Allchin 1958, 97).

Harriet Monsell (1811-1883) was the widow of the Reverend Charles Monsell. While he was studying for the priesthood in Oxford, the Oxford Movement influenced them both with its emphasis on reviving the catholic tradition in the Church of England. Following her husband's death in 1850, Mrs. Monsell consecrated her life to the service of God as a member of the young Community of Saint John Baptist at Clewer, England, near Windsor. The Reverend Thomas T. Carter founded the community in 1851 and wrote

Fig. 2.40
Lancet Windows
south wall, center
dedicated May 11, 1956

Mother Harriet Monsell (r.)
20 in. x 110 in.

John Mason Neale (l.)
20 in. x 110 in.

its rule. Harriet Monsell was clothed as a novice on Ascension Day, 1851. Bishop Samuel Wilberforce received her profession of life vows on the Feast of Saint Andrew, November 30, 1852, making Mother Harriet the first Anglican Sister to be professed by a bishop (Anson 1955, 308ff). At the same time, she was installed as the first superior of the Community of Saint John Baptist.

Its foundational work was establishment of "penitentiaries" for the rescue of women trying to escape from prostitution. Under the direction of Mother Harriet, the young community grew, flourished, and expanded its work. Within five years, they established a home for children; twenty years later, by 1872, at least eighteen institutions, including several schools, had been built. Mission work began in India in 1874, the same year a school opened in Mendham, New Jersey (Anson 1955, 311).

Fig. 2.41
Mother Harriet Monsell Window
principal medallion – detail
Father Carter instructs Sisters.

In the lancet window, Mother Harriet is portrayed holding an open book (see figs. 2.40, 2.41). Above is the triumphant, risen Lamb of God, symbol of the Community of Saint John Baptist. Below a Sister is receiving a penitent girl, a portrayal of their first work. The principal medallion depicts Father Carter teaching the Sisters. The last one shows Saint John Baptist School in Mendham, New Jersey. The window text: "Commit the keeping of souls to Him" (1 Pet. 4:19).

John Mason Neale

John Mason Neale (1818-1864) founded the Society of Saint Margaret in 1855 at East Grinstead, England. He is well-known as a poet and a writer of hymns, among them "Good Christian men rejoice." Dr. Neale translated many Latin and Greek hymns, including "Come ye faithful, raise the strain," "All glory, laud and honor," and many of the Office hymns sung today by the Sisters of the Transfiguration and other religious communities.

As a priest, he actively supported the Oxford Movement in its revival of medieval liturgical forms, and was innovative in building on the foundations of the Oxford Movement leaders, a willingness that caused him some trouble. "At the same time he constantly stressed the importance of naturalness, and of avoiding any form of affectation or rigidity" (Allchin 1958, 97). Dr. Neale died on the Feast of the Transfiguration, August 6, 1864.

Fig. 2.42
John Mason Neale Window
principal medallion – detail
Dr. Neale writes hymns and poems.

The lancet window depicts Dr. Neale in Eucharistic vestments and holding an open book, signifying the Word of God for the world (see. Figs. 2.40, 2.42). Above is a cross of triumph, and below a scene showing the Saint Margaret Sisters' foundational work of nursing the poorest of the poor. The principal medallion shows Dr. Neale writing. In the medallion at the base are an ocean liner and the Statue of Liberty, depicting the arrival of the Saint Margaret Sisters in the United States in 1873. The window text: "The needy shall not ... be forgotten" (Ps. 9:18).

Mother Harriet
Mother Eva Mary

This set of windows was the first to be completed and installed. Mother Eva's window was the gift of former Bethany Home children who had known and loved her. Both windows were completed by August 6, 1948, in time for the celebration of the fiftieth anniversary of the founding of the Community of the Transfiguration.

MOTHER HARRIET (HARRIET STARR CANNON)
Harriet Starr Cannon (1823-1896) was born in Charleston, South Carolina. She was one of the "committee of five" foundresses of the first American religious community for women: the Community of Saint Mary in Peekskill, New York, founded in 1865.

The challenges of this early sisterhood were many and trying. In 1873, the Saint Mary Sisters established a school in Memphis, Tennessee, where they met with lukewarm acceptance or worse. However, attitudes toward them changed as a result of their work there during a devastating yellow fever epidemic in 1876. Many thousands of people fled the city, leaving the stricken to suffer and die untended. Some of the Saint Mary Sisters stayed to help. With their fellow workers, they provided heroic service among the sick and dying. Saint Mary Sisters Constance, Thecla, Ruth, and Frances died while ministering to the needy during this time. The Saint Mary Sisters were long remembered and extolled for their unselfish dedication. The high altar of Saint Mary's Episcopal Cathedral in Memphis is a tribute and memorial to them (Anson 1955, 558).

Fig. 2.43
Lancet Windows
south wall, east end
dedicated August 6, 1948
Feast of the Transfiguration

Mother Harriet (r.)
20 in. x 110 in.

Mother Eva Mary (l.)
20 in. x 110 in.

Mother Harriet is shown in the lancet window holding a book inscribed with a cross (see figs. 2.43, 2.44). Above is the anchor of hope because of her undaunted trust in the Lord and her faith that God would give grace to the Community of Saint Mary to persevere. Below is a girl, symbolizing their work with mountain girls of Tennessee through a boarding school at Sewanee, and with troubled girls in New York State. The principal medallion portrays Saint Mary Sisters nursing yellow fever patients in Memphis. The window text: "Yet is their hope full of immortality" (Wis. 3:4).

Fig. 2.44
Mother Harriet Window
principal medallion – detail
Sisters serve the sick and dying.

MOTHER EVA MARY (EVA LEE MATTHEWS)

The companion window commemorates Mother Eva Mary Matthews (1862-1928), foundress and first superior of the Community of the Transfiguration. Bishop Boyd Vincent of the Diocese of Southern Ohio authorized its founding. On August 6, 1898, the date celebrated as the founding of the Community, Eva Lee Matthews and Beatrice McCobb Henderson took their first vows.

The spirit of the Community as Mother Eva envisioned it is joyousness, which she saw exemplified in the Transfiguration of Christ, rather than rigid austerity. The Community of the Transfiguration was the first American Episcopal community to undertake foreign mission work, establishing Saint Lioba's Compound in Wuhu, China in 1914. Another essential characteristic of the Community of the Transfiguration has been and continues to be the use of the Offices from *The Book of Common Prayer*, making a clear and deliberate link between the Community and the daily life and worship of the Episcopal Church (Anson 1955, 563ff).

Many years before the foundation of the Community, Mother Eva had a dream that helped shape the future of the Community. Writing to her namesake niece, she said:

> I am going to tell you a dream that I had last night. I dreamed that I had a little baby in my arms, and it was not James Harlan nor you, but quite another baby, very white and beautiful, with strange, deep, sad eyes; and though it was quite dark in the room, there was so much light in his eyes that I could see him quite well, and I could feel him nestling so warm and soft against my breast and could hear him breathing softly and sweetly. And then some one in the dark whom I could not see began talking to me and said, 'It is the Christ Child you are holding, and if you will love and cherish Him, you may keep Him always.' and then I woke up, for it was morning. Wasn't that a lovely dream? (Cleveland 1929, 97)

Mother Eva's dream gave direction to her ideals for working with children, still a vital mission of the Community of the Transfiguration.

Fig. 2.45
Mother Eva Mary Window
principal medallion – detail
Mother Eva writes a story.

In the lancet window, Mother Eva is portrayed holding the Christ Child, as in her dream (see figs. 2.43, 2.45). Above her is the Star of Bethlehem. Below, a child symbolizes work of the Sisters of the Transfiguration in Lincoln Heights, a predominantly African-American neighborhood in Cincinnati. This work, originally called Saint Simon's Mission, was started soon after Mother Eva's death and continues today as Saint Monica's Recreation Center. In the principal medallion, Mother Eva is shown writing one of her numerous stories for the children of Bethany Home. In the last medallion is a Chinese Sister of the Transfiguration, commemorating Saint Lioba's Mission in China from 1914 to 1948. The window text: "In Thy light shall we see light" (Ps. 36:9).

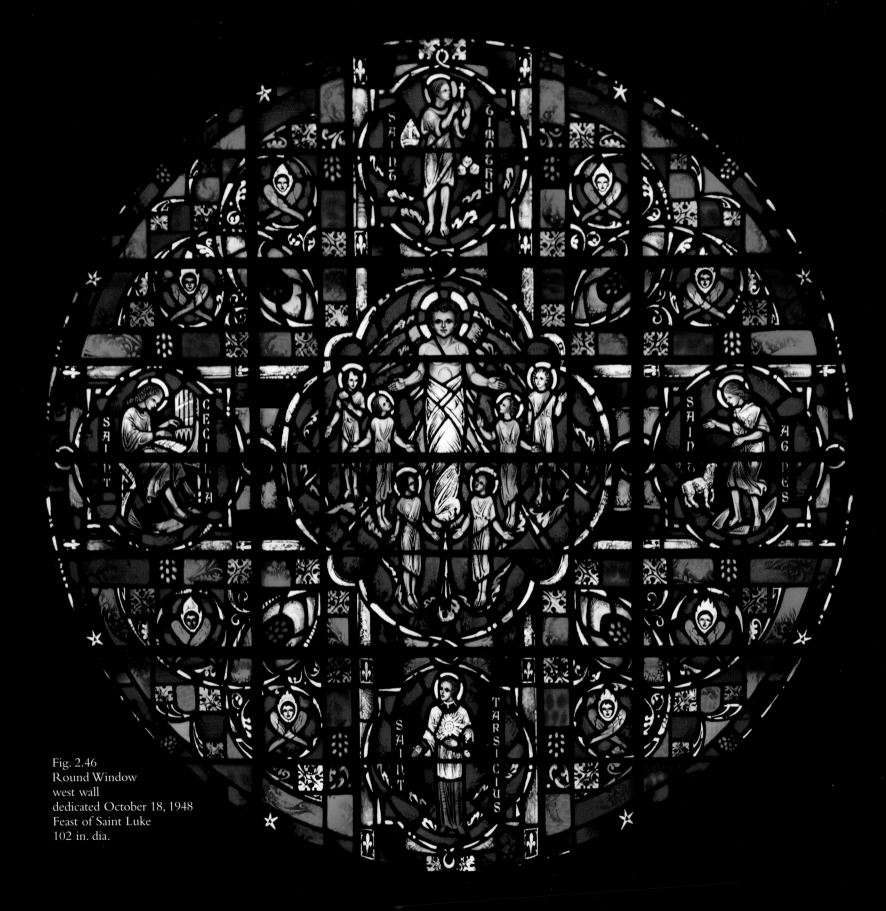

Fig. 2.46
Round Window
west wall
dedicated October 18, 1948
Feast of Saint Luke
102 in. dia.

The Round Window

The round stained glass window above the west entrance of the Chapel of the Transfiguration is often referred to as "the rose window," as are windows in a similar position in other churches. However, a closer look reveals that the leading in this window is that of a stylized Jerusalem Cross, the symbol of the Community, rather than the traditional rose pattern. Sister Beatrice referred to this window as "the eye of the church."

The round window is an excellent example of the brilliance and color typical of Connick glass. Darker than the lancet windows, the densely colored glass goes far to control the glare of the afternoon sun.

In keeping with the Community's commitment to the needs of children, the window is dedicated to childhood. The Infant Christ is featured in the central medallion. That image is surrounded by images of the Holy Innocents, killed by King Herod during his search for the Child. The four accompanying medallions, clockwise from the top, portray Saint Timothy, Saint Agnes, Saint Tarsicius, and Saint Cecilia – all of them Christian martyrs (see fig. 2.46).

Saint Timothy (d.c.97) is shown with a bishop's miter, reflecting his calling as Bishop of Ephesus. Timothy learned the Scriptures from his mother and grandmother, who were disciples of Saint Paul in Lystra. From his youth, Timothy was a coworker with Paul in the mission field. Timothy was stoned to death at Ephesus because he opposed a pagan festival in honor of the goddess Diana. The stones of his martyrdom are also shown in the window (Thurston 1956, 1:158).

Saint Agnes (d.c.303) is shown with a lamb. At the age of thirteen, Agnes was martyred for her faith during the persecutions under the rule of the Roman emperor Diocletian. She was condemned to be burned at the stake. Legend says that the flames died down as she prayed, so she was executed with a sword (Clarke 1968, 32).

Saint Tarsicius (d.c.255) is shown as a young acolyte. According to legend, he encountered an angry mob while carrying the Sacrament to prisoners. They asked what he was carrying and battered him to death when he would not give it up to them. Then, when they searched his body and clothing, no trace of the Sacrament could be found (Thurston 1956, 3:335).

Saint Cecilia (d.c.177), patron saint of music, is shown seated at an organ. A Roman girl raised as a Christian, Cecilia was forced by her father to marry a young man despite her vow of perpetual virginity. Her faith and loving witness was the cause of the conversion of her husband and his brother to Christianity. All three died violently at the hands of non-believers. Cecilia's courage and faith in the face of persecution and death are said to have been the cause of many conversions, including those of her executioners. Her patronage of music is attributed to the story that, on her wedding day, Cecilia sat silently apart from the guests, praying for help and singing to God in her heart (Thurston 1956, 4: 402).

A grapevine, symbolic of Christian unity and fruitfulness, outlines smaller medallions of blue-winged cherubs. White fleurs-de-lis, symbolizing purity, are sprinkled through the cross that is formed by the medallions. The five-pointed star of the New Testament enriches the outer border of the window.

"the eye of the church"

- Sister Beatrice

Mother Eva and Sister Beatrice planned for paintings to hang in the nave long before the Chapel was designed or built. During a trip to England in 1907, they visited various museums and galleries to select the art. They then either commissioned or purchased five full-sized copies of Renaissance paintings, the reproductions being executed by the well-known English artist Margaret Bernadine Hall (1863-1910). In a letter to one of the Sisters, Jane Sellars of the British National Museums and Galleries wrote that the artist was born in Liverpool, England and was the daughter of its mayor. She studied in Rome and Paris, where she lived from 1894 to 1907. She did most of her painting of portraits and genre subjects there.

The Hall copies include *The Mystery of the Immaculate Conception* (Murillo), *John the Baptist with Lamb* (Murillo), *The Holy Family* (Raphael), *Christ Bearing the Cross* (Ribalta), and *The Vision of Saint Helena* (Veronese). The only copy not done by Hall is *Jesus, The Virgin Mary, Saint Elizabeth and John the Baptist* (del Sarto), which was purchased from Closson's Art Gallery, Cincinnati, Ohio. One of the paintings in the nave is an original: *A Group of Saints* by Miguel Cabrera, which is on loan to the Community from the Episcopal Diocese of Southern Ohio.

For biographical information about the artists whose works hang in the Chapel, please see "Artists' Biographies."

Fig. 2.47
Jesus, the Virgin Mary, Saint Elizabeth and John the Baptist
by Andrea del Sarto
Painting (copy). 40 in. x 54¾ in.

Jesus, The Virgin Mary, Saint Elizabeth and John the Baptist by Andrea del Sarto (1486-1530) hangs on the north wall near the back (see fig. 2.47). In this family scene by a Florentine painter of the High Renaissance, Saint Mary holds Jesus on her lap and concentrates her attention on Him. The Child's eyes are on His older cousin, John, who is pointing to Jesus. John's hair is long and uncut, as would have been appropriate to one dedicated to God's service as a member of the ancient Order of Nazarites. Elizabeth, who is John's mother and Mary's cousin, watches over the three. The original painting hangs in the Pitti Palace in Florence, Italy.

The Mystery of the Immaculate Conception by Bartolome Estaban Murillo (1618-1682), a popular seventeenth century Spanish Baroque painter, hangs in the center of the north wall (see fig. 2.48). The inspiration for the painting is found in Revelation 12:1: "A great portent appeared in heaven: a woman clothed with the sun, with the moon under her feet, and on her head a crown of twelve stars." Traditionally this woman has been identified as Mary, the mother of Jesus. The woman, her feet resting on a crescent moon, is dressed in a flowing robe of white, the color traditionally associated with purity, innocence, and martyrdom. She has a blue mantle wrapped around her, blue being a color traditionally associated with Mary and representing both truth and eternity. Rather than the traditional halo, the woman's body seems to reflect the light of the sun, which, if it could be seen, would be directly behind her. Surrounding her are groups of cherubs. The original painting hangs in the Louvre Museum in Paris, France.

Fig. 2.48
The Mystery of the Immaculate Conception
by Bartolome Estaban Murillo
Painting (copy). 36½ in. x 53½ in.

John the Baptist with Lamb, also by Bartolome Estaban Murillo, hangs in the front of the nave on the north side (see fig. 2.49). This poignant painting is filled with scriptural allusion, contrasts of light and darkness, and a foreshadowing of coming events. Inspired by the proclamation attributed to the adult John: "Here is the Lamb of God who takes away the sin of the world!" (John 1:29), Murillo painted a chubby-cheeked child, at first glance untouched by evil. The lamb with whom the child is snuggling stands on a boulder under a large tree.

The child wears rough, torn clothing. The rock may represent the altar on which the ram was sacrificed in place of Isaac (Gen. 22:13). In the background, light shines faintly on a body of water, possibly representing the Jordan River. The original painting hangs in the National Gallery in London, England.

The Holy Family by Raphael (Raffaello Santi or Sanzio, 1483-1526), one of the greatest Italian Renaissance painters, hangs on the south wall of the nave near the font (see fig. 2.50). This domestic scene, as with many others, has layers of meaning. Jesus, a toddler, is leaping into Mary's arms and she reaches lovingly to catch Him, her eyes lowered. To their right, Elizabeth holds John protectively. He reaches toward Jesus. Tucked into the bend of John's arm is a simple cross. Joseph, traditionally the protector, is in the background, resting his head on his hand, and observing all that is going on. In the upper left are two angels, one holding a crown of flowers over Mary's head and the other looking on. Behind them is a small window, looking out on a pastoral landscape. The original hangs in the Metropolitan Museum of Art, New York.

Fig. 2.49
John the Baptist with Lamb
by Bartolome Estaban Murillo
Painting (copy). 53 ½ in. x 75 ½ in.

Fig. 2.50
The Holy Family
by Raphael
Painting (copy). 51 in. x 78 in.

Fig. 2.51
A Group of Saints
by Miguel Cabrera
Painting (original). 44 in. x 58 in.

Fig. 2.52
Christ Bearing the Cross
by Francisco Ribalta
Painting (copy). 46 in. x 84 ½ in.

A Group of Saints, an original painting by Miguel Cabrera (1695-1786), a Mexican Indian artist from Antequera (now Oaxaca), Mexico, hangs on the south wall near the back (see fig. 2.51). A beautiful, dark-haired woman with a delicate crown on her head and an aspergill in her hand may represent Mary, as she is robed in blue and white. She is looking back over her shoulder at a man in white monastic robes, who seems to be trying to explain something to her. Behind him, another monastic, with African features and darker robes, is reaching out supportively to the other man. This painting is on loan to the Community of the Transfiguration from the Episcopal Diocese of Southern Ohio.

Christ Bearing the Cross by Francisco Ribalta (1565-1628), a distinguished artist from Valencia, Spain, hangs on the west wall to the south of the doors (see fig 2.52). It is a dark painting with details that are difficult to discern without close examination under good light. Hall presumably copied the original painting before it had been cleaned of centuries of accretions, so some of Ribalta's message is obscured. It remains, however, a powerful statement of the horror and isolation of Jesus' last hours.

This painting is Ribalta's interpretation of a vision that came to Francisco Jeronimó Simó, a young Valencian priest. As Father Simó "passed through the Calle de Caballeros, he heard a raucous noise of trumpets. In the midst of a disorderly crowd, the pale disheveled Christ bowed under the weight of the Cross" (Darby 1938, 108).

In his book *Francisco Ribalta and His School*, art historian Delphine Fritz Darby describes the striking contrast between the weary, sensitive Christ with "the beautiful hands, unusually long and smooth," and the "coarse, florid, thick-armed figure of the trumpeter and the cruel, worldly soldier" (Darby 1938, 107). In the background are Jesus' grieving mother and the beloved disciple, John. The original hangs in the National Gallery in London, England.

The Vision of Saint Helena, on the west wall north of the doors, was painted by Paolo Veronese (1528-1588), an Italian Renaissance painter of the Venetian school (see fig 2.53). It recounts the legend that Helena, mother of the Emperor Constantine, was given a command in a dream to travel to the Holy Land and recover the cross on which Jesus died. In her dream, she saw a cross held by two angels (Clarke 1968, 155). At age eighty, she did go to the Holy Land. The painting shows a young Helena, either resting or in deep contemplation, against a large window. She is richly dressed, as befits the mother of an emperor. In the evening twilight, two cherubs present a cross to her. A friend of the Community who has seen the original painting in London reports that it is far lighter and brighter than the one in the Chapel. The original was cleaned after Margaret Hall made this copy. The original hangs in the National Gallery in London, England.

Fig. 2.53
The Vision of Saint Helena
by Paolo Veronese
Painting (copy). 46 in. x 78 in.

Fig. 2.54
Singing Cherubs
by Luca della Robbia
Frieze (copy). 30 in. x 90 in.

Fig. 2.55
Madonna in Adoration
by Andrea della Robbia
Terra cotta (copy). 20 in. x 32 in.

OTHER ART IN THE NAVE

A number of pieces in the Chapel are copies of the work of master Italian Renaissance sculptors: Luca della Robbia (1400-1482) and Andrea della Robbia (1435-1525). The *Singing Cherubs* frieze above the west door is cast possibly from an original Luca della Robbia sculpture in bas relief (see fig. 2.54). The frieze was moved to the Chapel from the former Convent oratory.

Bambino, hanging by the south transept door over the baptismal font, was also moved from the former Convent oratory (see fig. 2.56). Andrea della Robbia made a series of ten glazed terra cotta bas relief, framed tondos of infants in swaddling clothes on a blue background for the Foundling Hospital in Florence, Italy. This is a copy of one of those bambinos.

Directly above the north transept door is another Andrea della Robbia copy. This glazed terra cotta bas relief sculpture is entitled *Madonna in Adoration* (see fig. 2.55). A young Madonna kneels prayerfully and looks down at her baby, who lies on the ground. Lilies adorn the scene. In the sky are two cherubs, and two hands hold a crown over her head.

One authority claims that the original is in the National Museum of Bargello in Florence, Italy. Another believes that the original is an unglazed terra cotta in the collection of the National Gallery of Art in Washington, D.C.

In a wall niche to the left of *Madonna in Adoration* stands *Saint Michael and the Dragon*, designed by the Chapel architect, Dr. Ralph Adams Cram (see fig. 2.57). The statue was carved in Italy of Carrara marble especially for the Community. Saint Michael was selected as patron saint of Bethany School. One of the four archangels, Saint Michael is traditionally identified as the leader of the armies of heaven, the one who led the fight with Satan and cast the evil one from heaven. Wearing a coat of armor, Saint Michael holds the point of a spear against the defeated dragon's head as the dragon lies at his feet.

Fig. 2.56
Bambino
by Andrea della Robbia
Terra cotta (copy). 32 in. x 40 in.

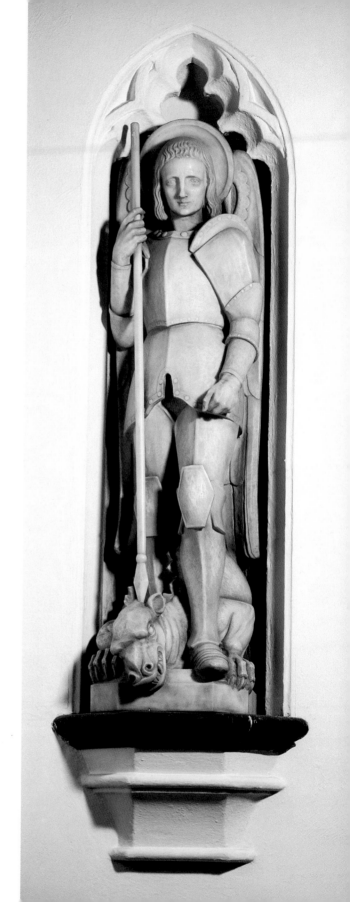

Fig. 2.57
Saint Michael and the Dragon
Marble (original). 48 in. (height)

Fig. 2.58
The Transfiguration
Icon on stone.
(original). 8 in. x 13 in.

An almost hidden work of art hangs on the east wall of the nave, to the left of the rood screen and behind the Assistant Superior's stall. In a glass-fronted, wooden box frame is *The Transfiguration*, painted on a small stone from Mt. Tabor by Sister Alexis of the Russian Orthodox Visitation Convent in Ain Karim, near Jerusalem (see fig 2.58). Ain Karim is said to be where Elizabeth and Zachariah, parents of John the Baptist, lived.

Adjacent to this painting is the brass processional cross with the engraved motto, "And they follow the Lamb wheresoever he goeth." The cross is used most frequently for Bethany School worship services.

The white marble baptismal font was moved from the former Convent oratory to the south wall under *Bambino* (see fig. 2.59). An oak lid covers the 16-inch octagonal bowl; it has a brass ring held by a brass plate in the shape of a Jerusalem Cross. The letters "IHS" are carved in one of the eight faces of the bowl. In 1926, Sister Beatrice brought the three stones embedded in the bowl from the Jordan River; they were taken from the traditional place of Jesus' baptism (see fig. 2.60).

Fig. 2.60
Baptismal Font Bowl
Marble.

Fig. 2.59
Baptismal Font
Marble. 16 in. x 37 in.

The chancel, including the choir and the sanctuary, is the center of liturgy and devotion in the Chapel.

The magnificent black walnut rood screen with its pillars and the principal figures of Calvary separates the nave and the chancel (see fig. 2.61). The pillars of the rood screen symbolize "a sustaining power, a bridge between lower and higher levels, earth and spirit" (Whone 1977, 132). A life-sized crucifix with Christ's head lowered to the right, symbolizing the cross of suffering and death, surmounts the center of the rood screen. Flanking the cross are the figures of Saint Mary, His mother, and Saint John, the beloved disciple. Figures of eleven apostles, equally spaced, stand below on the cross beam of the screen. A traditional symbol of the apostle accompanies each figure. Behind each figure, facing the choir, is a figure of the respective apostle's guardian angel holding a musical instrument. Each apostle and his angel are fastened together to prevent them from falling due to the vibration of the organ. Fritz Abplanalp carved the apostle and angel figures on site. Craftsmen of the Casson Company carved the rest of the rood screen, including the cross and figures.

Figures of the Apostles

The rood screen includes figures of eleven apostles, with names inscribed on the base (see fig. 2.61). Each apostle holds a symbol that traditionally represents him. From left to right, they are:

Matthew — *book*

Andrew — *cross in his right hand, scroll in his left*

Paul — *sword in his right hand, scroll in his left*

James of Jerusalem — *staff*

James — *pilgrim's staff*

Jude — *praying*

Peter — *key*

Philip — *staff*

Bartholomew — *stone*

Simon — *saw*

Thomas — *carpenter's square in his left hand*

Fig. 2.61
Rood Screen
Wood.
Apostles 21 in. (height)
Angels 18 in. (height)

Fig. 2.62
Ambo
Wood. 60 in. (height)
Evangelist Figures 7 in. (height)

Choir

The choir, the part of the chancel closest to the nave, is raised three steps above the level of the nave. The floor is Vermont antique green marble and gray Tennessee marble in a checkerboard pattern (see fig. 2.61).

AMBO

The ambo stands in the center, a two-sided pedestal that holds the Old Testament on one side and the New Testament on the other (see fig. 2.62). The ambo replaces the usual pulpit and lectern and rotates for convenience when the Scriptures are being read. Ambos are customary in a monastic chapel, where services are conducted primarily for the members of the choir.

Fritz Abplanalp did the elaborate ambo carvings. Wheat and grapes form the border around the ambo. On the upright support are small figures of the four evangelists, similar to the monk and nun figures on the altar (see fig. 2.63). A sharp-eyed visitor concluded that the three bearded figures were the Jewish Matthew, Mark, and John, while the fourth was the Greek Luke, whose countrymen did not wear beards at that time.

In the center of the Old Testament side is a six-pointed Star of David, the symbol of Judaism (see fig. 2.64). In the center of the star is a Menorah. The Hebrew word for Lord is inscribed beneath the star. This side of the ambo includes a symbol in each corner: a lamp denoting Wisdom, the Tables of the Law, a scroll commemorating the Prophets, and a harp denoting the Psalms of David.

The surface of the New Testament side portrays the Lamb of God (see fig. 2.65). The Lamb carries a banner with a Jerusalem Cross, symbolizing the triumphant, risen Christ. Surrounding this image are the seals of the dioceses where the Community had worked for at least ten years by the year 1929: Ohio, Southern Ohio, North Carolina, Hawaii, and China. After 1955, California and Puerto Rico were added. Below these, inscribed in Greek, are the words "Jesus Christ."

Fig. 2.63
Altar – detail
Nun and Monk Figures
9 in. (height)

Fig. 2.64
Ambo – Old Testament Side
Wood. 25 in. x 25 in.
Carved lower border 2 3/4 in.

Fig. 2.65
Ambo – New Testament Side
Wood. 25 in. x 25 in.
Carved lower border 2 3/4 in.

Fig. 2.67
Altar Retable – detail

Fig. 2.68
Choir Stall – detail
Angel Head

Fig. 2.66
Choir Stalls and Assistant
Superior's Stall (left)

CHOIR STALLS

The choir stalls, made of black walnut by Robert Mitchell Manufacturing Company, provide seating for forty Sisters. Each of the three tiers of stalls is one step higher from the middle pavement (see fig. 2.66). There are four special stalls, two of them next to the rood screen on either side of the choir. Three are for the Superior, Assistant Superior, and the Novice Guardian. The Sister-in-charge of Bethany Home occupied the fourth stall when there were boarders in attendance at Chapel service and a supervisory eye was required. Now, however, the fourth stall is used for the lectors and intercessor at the Eucharist.

On the parapets and back of each row of stalls, Fritz modified the retable carvings (see fig. 2.67). On each side of the choir, on the canopy above and across the back seats, are two rows with nine angel heads each (see fig. 2.68). These repeat the motif of angel heads from the lower corners of the reredos and represent choirs of angels praising God. The upper row is said to resemble Fritz Abplanalp's daughter and the lower row Sister Marion Beatrice as a postulant, although there is some speculation whether they served as models.

The choir houses some of Fritz Abplanalp's most intricate and beautiful carvings. They are unique features of the Chapel of the Transfiguration, and merit special attention. First, Fritz's highly visible, carved medallions of New Testament scenes grace the panels behind the organ, the stalls of the Superior and Assistant Superior, and the top, back row of stalls on each side (see fig. 2.69). His detailed, sensitive execution of these scenes is remarkable (see fig. 2.71). Then, there is the hidden beauty of the misericords on the underseats of the back rows of stalls, which portray events from the Old Testament that correspond to the New Testament scenes on the panels above them. A misericord is a narrow ledge on the underside of a hinged choir seat. With the seat turned up, a choir member, while standing, can lean against the misericord.

The misericord under the Superior's seat is an intricate scene of King David, seated on his throne and holding a harp (II Sam. 2:4) (see fig. 2.70). To the left are three sheep, recalling David's early life as a shepherd. To the right is a lion that David killed in protecting his sheep. The medallion above the Superior's seat portrays Jesus Christ, the descendant of David, reigning in glory (see fig. 2.71). The misericord under the Assistant Superior's seat presents a scene where an angel appeared to the parents of Samson to tell them they would have a son (Judg.13:3). In the medallion above the Assistant Superior's seat, the Archangel Gabriel appears to the Virgin Mary with the message that she has been chosen by God to be the Mother of Our Lord (Luke 1: 31).

The misericords present a total of fifteen handsomely crafted scenes, all of them hidden under the choir seats.

Fig. 2.69
Superior's Choir Stall
30 in. x 158 in.

Fig. 2.70
Misericord – King David
under Superior's choir seat
8 in. x 15 in.

Choir Panels and Misericords

Fritz Abplanalp, the Swiss woodcarver who worked on site during the early years of the Chapel, carved intricate medallions of New Testament scenes into the panels behind the organ and all the stalls in the choir. Under each seat in the back rows of the choir is a misericord – a narrow ledge that includes a beautiful woodcarving of an event in the Old Testament corresponding to the New Testament panel above the seat. Abplanalp carved all the misericords.

The following list of panels and misericords begins on the north side of the choir, with the seat nearest the bell rope, and ends on the south side, near the priest's chair.

Panel	**Misericord**
1. *The Nativity (Luke 2:11)*	*Adam and Eve (Gen. 3:6)*
2. *The Presentation (Luke 2:22)*	*Samuel taken to Shiloh (1 Sam. 1:24)*
3. *Flight into Egypt (Matt. 2:13)*	*Joseph sold into slavery in Egypt (Gen. 37:28)*
4. *Jesus in the temple (Luke 2:46-47)*	*Joseph reveals himself to his brothers (Gen. 45:4)*
5. *Baptism of Jesus (Matt. 3:13)*	*Noah's Ark (Gen. 6:14)*
6. *Temptation of Jesus (Matt. 4:1)*	*Worship of the Golden Calf (Exod. 32:8)*
7. *Sermon on the Mount (Matt. 5:1)*	*Ten Commandments (Exod. 20:7-17)*
8. *Miracle at Cana (John 2:1)*	*Elisha and the widow's debt (2 Kings 4:1)*
9. *Raising of Lazarus (John 11:1, 43-44)*	*Elisha raises the Shunammite's son (2 Kings 4:34)*
10. *Last Supper (Matt. 26:17)*	*Manna in the wilderness (Exod. 16:15)*
11. *Jesus in Gethsemane (Matt. 26:36)*	*Angel appears to Daniel (Dan. 6:22, 9:21)*
12. *The Crucifixion (Matt. 27:35)*	*[organ]*
13. *The Resurrection (Matt: 28:7)*	*[organ]*
14. *The Great Commission (Matt. 28: 19-20)*	*[organ]*
15. *The Ascension (Acts 1:9)*	*Elijah's ascent into heaven (2 Kings 2:11)*
16. *Pentecost (Acts 2:1-3)*	*Tower of Babel (Gen. 11:7)*

The panel of the Superior's stall portrays Jesus Christ on the Throne, and the misericord under the seat portrays David as King (2 Sam. 2:4).

The panel of the Assistant Superior's stall portrays the Annunciation (Luke 1:31), and the misericord under the seat presents Samson's birth foretold (Judg. 13:3).

Fig. 2.71
Medallion – Jesus Christ
above Superior's choir seat
9 in. x 14½ in.

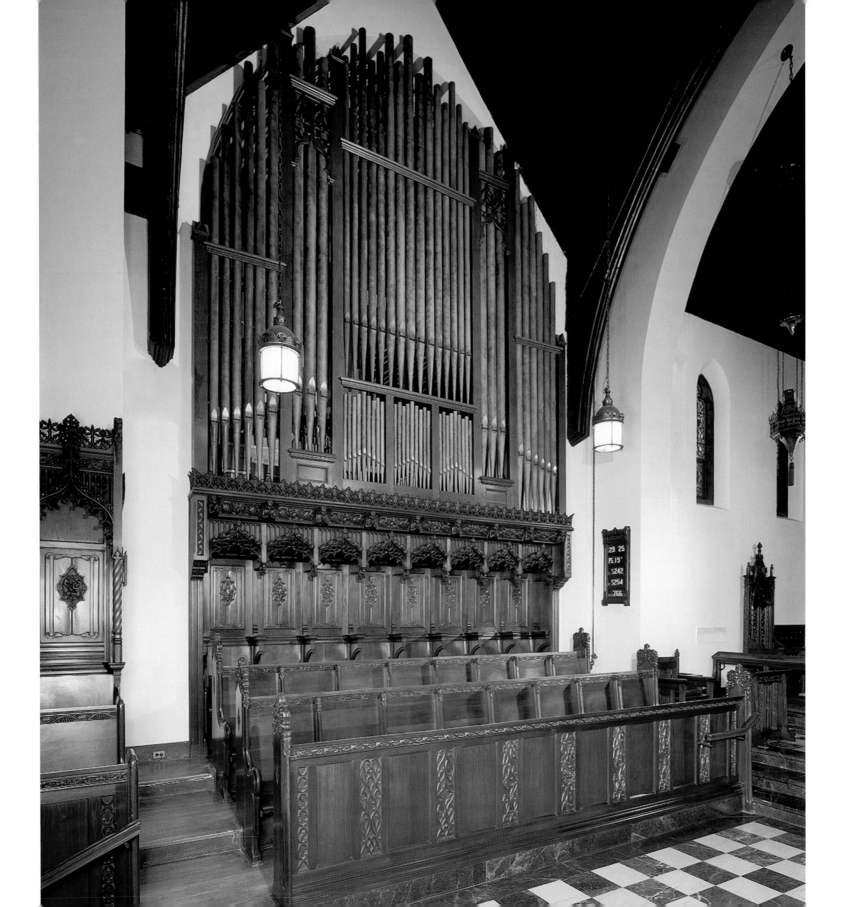

Organ

The Möller Organ Company, Hagerstown, Maryland built the original Chapel organ. It was designed especially for women's and children's voices by Harold Frederick and John Prower Symons, a fellow in the American Guild of Organists (FAGO). A local church organist, Symons was very interested in the music programs at Bethany Home and the Convent. On Saturday, June 8, 1929, for the First Evensong of the Sunday before the consecration of the Chapel, Symons played the hymn "Praise God From Whom All Blessings Flow" – the first hymn played on the Chapel organ.

Many years later, when the Möller organ needed extensive repair, the Sisters decided to replace it with a new instrument. In spring, 1977, it was replaced with a Schantz organ, built by the Schantz Organ Company, Orrville, Ohio and designed by Roger Heather, an organ architect. It was first played during the service on Easter Sunday, 1977 (see fig. 2.72).

The Schantz organ has 1,835 pipes, 40 stops and 28½ ranks. There are four complete divisions (great, swell, choir, pedal) and a keyboard of three manuals with a tracker touch. The console, made of walnut, was designed to match the carved wood.

The sound of the organ is extremely flexible and lends itself to music of all periods and composers. Its tone is clear and bright, the result of applying basic principles of good tonal structure, employing low wind pressure, functional pipe scaling, and sensitive voicing of the registers. In addition, the inclusion of some colorful romantic registers lends versatility to the instrument. It was tonally finished by Robert Maye, a flue voicer, from Akron, Ohio.

At the dedication service on April 17, 1977, Mr. Heather presented a varied program to show the instrument's capabilities, with compositions by the Bach family, Sigfrid Karg-Elert, Charles-Marie Widor and American composers William Selby and Dudley Buck. Three additional dedication recitals took place: Debra Dunn, May 8, 1977; Richard Silbereis, May 29, 1977; and Ritter Werner, June 11, 1977.

In October, 1983, Mr. Maye, realizing that the great division had too much volume for the Sisters' musical needs, set up a small voicing machine in the great division and softened the whole division to create a gentler sound. In the late 1980s, he made and installed a cymbalstern, with four bells of different pitches, in the organ. The word cymbalstern means "bell star." When a stop is turned on, two lead weights rotate and strike the bells in a random pattern.

Over the years, a number of gifted organists have accompanied the Sisters in worship services, as well as presented recitals. From the beginning, there have been Sister organists, the first being Sister Ruth Magdalene, who also became a very accomplished carillonneur. The following Sisters have also been organists: Angela Hannah, Virginia Cecilia, Paula Irene, Hilary Mary, Leinaala Josephine, Elizabeth Anne, Monica Mary, and Marcia Frances.

Other organists have included Christopher Alvin Morgan; Richard Silbereis; Parvin Titus, FAGO; and Ritter Warner, FAGO. Since 1981, John Austin Deaver, DMA, has been organist and choir director.

Fig. 2.72
Choir Stalls and Organ Pipes

Fig. 2.73
Christ the Pantocrator
Icon. 6 in. x 7 ½ in. (inside frame)

Two Russian icons are displayed in the choir: Christ as Pantocrator and the Virgin and Child as Theotokos Hodigitria. There are thousands of variations of both. Most Russian cities have their own distinctive designs for the Theotokos Hodigitria.

In the Christus Pantocrator icon on the wall adjacent to the Assistant Superior's stall, Christ is depicted with a solemn, rigid, ascetic full face and dark eyes that look straight out at the viewer (see 2.73). The figure is half-length, with the right hand raised in blessing and the left hand holding a Bible open to a Greek version of John 13:34: "Just as I have loved you, you also should love one another." In Russian are the words "for Lord Almighty." The halo and background are gold, symbolizing the glory of heaven. The icon is inscribed with the Greek monogram for Jesus Christ (Wild 1961, plate 17).

The icon on the corresponding wall adjacent to the Superior's stall is the Theotokos Hodigitria of Tikhvin. The Virgin Mary is shown with a rigid, flat, solemn face turned toward the Child, giving her a sense of softness and adoration (see fig. 2.74). A half-length figure, she holds Jesus in her arms, against her left shoulder, with her right hand pointing to Him. Jesus raises His right hand in blessing, and His bare feet show out from the folds of His garment (Quenot 1991, 45).

The elaborately designed halos and clothing are of rich gold and silver, which is a variation from other icons of the Virgin of Tikhvin. A votive candle hangs on a chain attached to the top of the frame. It is lighted on feasts of the Virgin.

Sanctuary

The sanctuary of any church is its most sacred space. It is here that the Eucharistic liturgy is celebrated, the Sacrament is reserved, and worshipers come to receive Communion.

The sanctuary of the Chapel of the Transfiguration is approached by a series of steps (see fig. 2.75). Three steps lead from the choir level to the altar rail, which separates the choir from the sanctuary. The sanctuary is then one step higher. Three more steps lead to the high altar, the focal point of sacramental worship in the Chapel.

Fritz Abplanalp carved the altar rail in place, applying his familiar motif of grapes and wheat (see fig. 2.76). That motif appears again on the priests' chairs, situated in front of the altar rail on either side. Directly above, three sanctuary lights hang from an arch in the ceiling. The center one is always lit, signifying the Presence of Christ in the Reserved Sacrament on the altar. During celebrations of the Eucharist on Sundays and special feast days, all three sanctuary lights are lit.

Fig. 2.74
Theotokos Hodigitria of Tikhvin
Icon. 12 ½ in. x 14 in. (framed)

Fig. 2.76
Altar Rail
7 ¼ in. x 121 in.
28 in. (height)

Fig. 2.75
Sanctuary
Reredos 12 ft. x 22 ft.
Altar with Retables 8 ft. x 5 ft.
Crucifix 9 ½ in. x 21 in.
Candlesticks 18 in. (height)
Painting 6 ft. x 9 ft.

Fig. 2.78
Mosaic in Mensa
12 ½ in. x 16 ½ in. (framed)

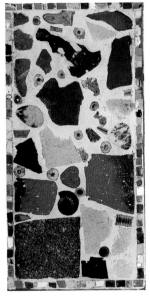

Fig. 2.79
Mosaic in Footpace
8 in. x 16 in. with border

MAIN ALTAR

Crafted of century-old oak salvaged from a French chateau, the altar was constructed and carved in Paris in 1919 by Arthur Nieb. The front carvings portray Jesus blessing little children, Jesus with Mary and Martha at Bethany, and Mary anointing the feet of Jesus (see fig. 2.77). The crucifix, with its corpus of hand-carved ivory, and the six candlesticks, finished with gold leaf, are made from the same salvaged oak as the altar.

A mosaic set into the mensa, the top of the altar, is made of small stones that Sister Beatrice brought from the Holy Land in 1926 (see fig. 2.78). One tiny black stone came from the site of Pilate's judgment hall, and Jesus' feet may have touched it. Around the edge of the mosaic is a gold band engraved with the names of the places from which each stone was collected.

Directly in front of the altar, embedded in the footpace, is a mosaic of stones that Mother Eva and Sister Beatrice brought from English and Scottish holy places in 1907 (see fig. 2.79). The specific locations are noted in a photograph hanging in the narthex. Mother Eva received the mosaic glass used in the border from the verger at Saint Paul's Cathedral, where repair work was being done in the dome.

Of these two mosaics, Sister Mariya Margaret wrote: "By means of these two mosaics of stone, we may say that at Mass the Blessed Sacrament stands on the Holy Land, and the priest stands upon the Church of England, our Mother Church." (Mariya 1979)

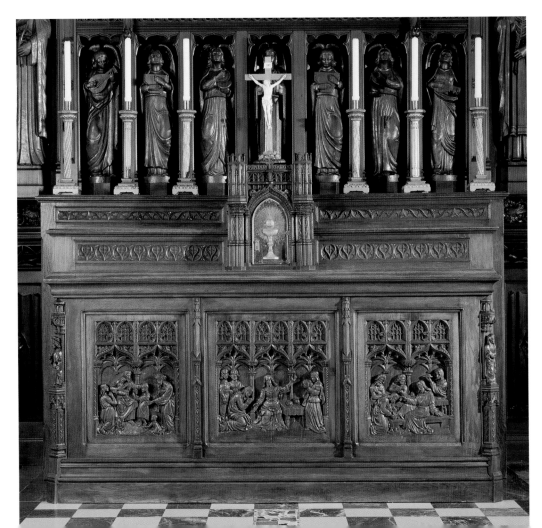

Fig. 2.77
Altar

During the Service of Consecration on June 11, 1929, marble mason Otto Kadon engraved a Maltese cross in the footpace as a seal of consecration.

According to custom, the bodies of founders and foundresses are buried under the altars of their communities. The village council of Glendale, Ohio passed a special ordinance to allow for Mother Eva Mary's burial in the Chapel of the Transfiguration. The body of Mother Eva was interred under the altar June 12, 1929, the day following the Consecration of the Chapel. Engraved in the marble floor under the altar are the words:

The Rev. Mother Foundress Eva Mary
"The virgins that be her fellows shall bear her company
and shall be brought unto thee." (Ps. 45:14)

A magnificent black walnut reredos, made by the Casson Company, frames the altar and the painting of the Transfiguration that hangs above it (see fig. 2.75).

Dr. Cram, the Chapel architect, suggested to artist Lee Woodward Zeigler (1868-1952) the El Greco-like style of the Transfiguration painting (see fig. 2.80). Zeigler was commissioned for the work and installed the original himself. In the painting, Jesus, with light from within and above, stands between the prophets Moses, who is holding the commandment tablets, and Elijah, who is holding a scroll. Both look to Jesus. Kneeling in the foreground on the left are Peter and James, and on the right is John.

Fritz Abplanalp carved the fifteen angels within the reredos on site. The seven angels on the bottom row of the reredos hold musical instruments with the exception of the middle one, who holds a crown. Next to the painting are four praying angels; the upper two have their hands together, the lower two hold censors. The four larger angels represent the archangels, and each one carries a symbol traditionally associated with that angel (see fig. 2.81):

- The Archangel Gabriel holds a lily, representing the Annunciation (lower left);
- The Archangel Raphael bears a cup used to comfort Jesus in Gethsemane (upper left);
- The Archangel Michael has a flaming, fiery sword (upper right);
- The Archangel Uriel holds a palm branch, symbolizing the martyrs and victory over death in the Resurrection. (lower right)

Four pieces of wood from the original coffin of Saint Cuthbert are set in the reredos behind the retable of the altar. Mother Eva and Sister Beatrice brought them from Durham Cathedral in England in 1907. The relics are enclosed in a gold and silver box, given by Bishop Paul Matthews.

Fig. 2.80
Transfiguration
by Lee Woodward Zeigler
Painting (original.) 6 ft. x 9 ft.

Fig. 2.81
Altar – detail
Four Archangels: Gabriel (left), Raphael, Michael, and Uriel

Fig. 2.82
Virgin Mary Window
north wall of sanctuary
dedicated March 25, 1949
12 in. x 69¼ in.

Fig. 2.83
St. Elizabeth Window
south wall of sanctuary
dedicated June, 1952
12 in. x 69¼ in.

SANCTUARY WINDOWS

The five stained glass windows in the sanctuary were among the last to be installed in the Chapel. These windows were created by Riordan Stained Glass Studio, Cincinnati, Ohio. It is easy to see a distinct difference in their style, as contrasted to the style of the nave windows. Sister Beatrice wanted to employ Riordan Studio in order to encourage young local talent. Unfortunately, one of the artists who designed these windows died shortly after the first two were completed.

Virgin Mary Window

Hung on the north wall beside the reredos, the Virgin Mary window portrays Mary holding the Child Jesus (see fig. 2.82). It includes an upper medallion of the Annunciation, showing the Archangel appearing to Mary. Above that is a descending dove, the Holy Spirit. The lower medallion pictures the Fall. Adam and Eve are standing in the Garden of Eden with the serpent entwined in the tree of knowledge of good and evil. In the left lower corner is an apple from which two bites are taken. Symbols in the border are the fleurs-de-lis of purity, the symbolic "IHS" for Jesus, the letters "MR" for Maria Regina, and the five-pointed Star of Bethlehem.

This window is commonly referred to as the Virgin Mary window, although no name appears on the window itself.

Saint Elizabeth Window

The Saint Elizabeth window hangs on the south wall of the sanctuary (see fig. 2.83). Elizabeth is shown with her son, John the Baptist, holding the long-stemmed cross – his special symbol. In the medallion above is the Visitation of the Virgin Mary to Elizabeth. The medallion below shows the angel appearing to Zachariah in the temple to tell him he would have a son. In the border are the fleurs-de-lis of purity, the baptismal shell, the lamp of prophecy, "Z" for Zachariah and "E" for Elizabeth. In the left lower corner is the star of David for Zachariah, the temple priest, and in the right corner is a Maltese cross, representing Christ.

This window is commonly referred to as the Saint Elizabeth window, although no name appears on the window itself.

Saint Anne Window

The other window in the south wall represents Saint Anne, mother of Saint Mary (see fig. 2.84). Anne is teaching her child to read. Mary's hair is held in place with a band of Christmas roses, symbolizing the nativity of Jesus. Above is a crown and below a nest of baby birds, symbolizing Saint Anne's nurturing motherhood. The name "St. Anne" appears on the window.

Windows of Mary and Martha of Bethany

The Sisters intended for the two remaining windows in the north wall to portray Mary and Martha of Bethany, both of whom are especially significant in the ethos of the Community. However, an unfortunate conflict occurred in which Mary of Bethany was identified as Mary Magdalene. This was a common notion at the time the windows were designed, but which most contemporary scholars would now reject. The window labeled "St. M. Magdalene" actually represents Mary of Bethany, and it should have been so labeled.

The first window on the north side represents Martha of Bethany, shown as a busy homemaker holding a ladle and keys attached to a cincture (see fig. 2.85). Above her is the torch, bearing the light of truth from age to age. Below is a dragon with its jaws tied shut, a symbol for Satan and depiction of the legend that Martha overcame a dragon. The companion window shows Mary of Bethany holding the container of ointment from which some traditions say that she anointed the feet of Jesus (see fig. 2.86). Below is a rowboat, symbolizing a ninth century legend of Mary of Bethany in which Mary, Martha, and Lazarus travel as missionaries in a boat with no rudder or sail that lands in Marseilles, France. In the legend, Mary reputedly dies thirty years later in a cave nearby.

Fig. 2.84
St. Anne Window
south wall of sanctuary
dedicated February, 1954
20¼ in. x 69¾ in.

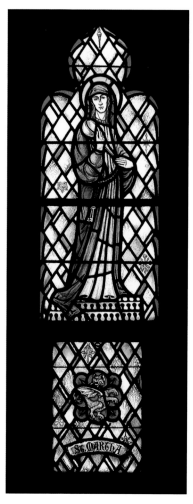

Fig. 2.85
St. Martha Window
north wall of sanctuary
dedicated February, 1954
20¼ in. x 69¾ in.

Fig. 2.86
St. M. Magdalene Window
north wall of sanctuary
dedicated February, 1954
20¼ in. x 69¾ in.

Fig. 2.87
Credence Table   32 ½ in. (height)
Candlesticks   26 in. (height)
Thurible   12 in. (height)
Thurible stand   57 in. (height)
Sanctus bell   7 in. dia.

SANCTUARY FURNITURE

On the credence table to the right of the altar are two brass Eucharistic candlesticks and a brass missal stand (see fig. 2.87). Nearby is a brass thurible and stand and a sanctus bell, which is rung at the time of the Consecration during the Eucharist.

The bishop's chair sits on the north side of the sanctuary (see fig. 2.88). Two small figures, representing Bishop Paul Matthews and Bishop Irving P. Johnson, stand one on each top corner of the chair back. Each holds a crozier made from old silver spoons from Mother Eva's family. A Jerusalem Cross is carved in bas relief on the upper portion of the chair back. Below the cross is a miter, symbolizing the line of succession of bishops from the apostles. A crozier, symbolic of pastoral care, and keys, symbolic of bishops' power of absolution, are also carved on the back panel of the chair.

Other sanctuary furnishings include a clergy chair with prie-dieu and two benches, which give a suggestion of sedilias, one on each side of the sanctuary.

All this furniture is black walnut and made by Robert Mitchell Company. It features carvings by Fritz Alpanalp, the talented, young Swiss woodcarver whose extensive artistic influence on the Chapel of the Transfiguration is unmistakable. In fact, the credence table was Fritz's first work.

Fig. 2.88
Bishop's Chair
30 in. x 24 in. x 96 in.
Carved figures   8 in. (height)

Priests' Sacristy

The priests' sacristy is a small room located in the east corner of the south arm of the cruciform Chapel. It serves as a vesting place for the celebrant and storage for a considerable number of vestments and religious items used in Chapel liturgical services.

VESTMENTS AND LINENS

A large cabinet on the south wall contains both old and new vestments, such as copes, chasubles, and dalmatics worn during Eucharistic celebrations. Many of them are in sets – that is, two or more vestments made from the same bolt of fabric and decorated in like manner. Some of these are of special interest: remarkable for their age, beauty, history, or connection to valued traditions.

A number of the vestments were made in Wuhu, China from 1914 to 1940, when the Sisters ministered to the local community at Saint Lioba's Compound. At True Light Industrial Facility, one of the Sisters' ministries, local women could earn money through the sale of handmade articles. The vestments acquired from Saint Lioba's Compound over the years exemplify the exquisite workmanship and skill of these women (see fig. 2.89). An especially impressive chasuble is made of plum-colored Japanese silk with an embroidered crucifix on the back (see fig. 2.90).

The Sisters of Saint Margaret in East Grinstead, England made the white vestment set traditionally used for Christmas, Easter, and the Feast of the Transfiguration. Mother Eva and Sister Beatrice ordered this set, including chasuble, stole, matching chalice veil, and burse, when they visited England in 1907. Sisters of the Holy Nativity repaired the set in 1960, and in 1991 the orphreys were restored and placed on new fabric. On the front is a pelican, a symbol of Christ's atonement for sin (see fig. 2.91). Legend, based on ancient beliefs, has it that, in times of famine, the pelican tears open her breast and feeds her young with her own blood. The Good Shepherd is the subject of the orphrey design on the back of the chasuble. (see fig. 2.92).

Sister Madeleine Mary, an expert seamstress and practicing physician, made the set of white satin vestments with blue velvet orpheys. They were first worn at the Service of Consecration, a Solemn High Eucharist. Mother Eva's sister, Mrs. Horace Gray, contributed the heavy satin from her wedding gown. The blue velvet orpheys were made from one of her trousseau gowns. This extensive, nine-piece set consists of chasuble, tunicle, dalmatic, stoles for those three items, and a cope. There is also a matching chalice veil and burse.

Fig. 2.89
Chasuble (back)
by Women of
St. Lioba's Compound
Silk damask.

Fig. 2.90
Chasuble (back)
by Women of
St. Lioba's Compound
Japanese silk.

Fig. 2.91
Chasuble (front)
with Pelican Orphrey
Silk damask.

Fig. 2.92
Chasuble (back)
with Good Shepherd Orphrey
Silk damask.

Fig. 2.93
Venetian Lace Frontal – detail

Two other sets of vestments are used for major feasts. Carolyn Campbell, an Associate, made the first, a twelve-piece set of white vestments with blue velvet orphreys, in 1979. It includes two chasubles, four stoles, one cope, a miter, two chalice veils, and two burses. There is also a set of white vestments – chasuble, stole, cope, chalice veil, and burse – with coronation tapestry orphreys, which is also used for major feasts.

Opposite the very full vestment cupboard is a tall chest of drawers, containing fair linens for the altar, smaller pieces for the credence table, and frontals for the altars. Four pieces are of special note:

- A blue velvet altar cover, embellished with a painted garland of pink and white flowers, was made by Sister Alexis of the Russian Orthodox Visitation Convent in Ain Karim, near Jerusalem (see figs. 2.93, 2.94);
- A frontal of heavy Venetian lace, reputed to be from the seventeenth century, was brought from England by Sister Ada Julian. It is often used in combination with the velvet altar cover on feast days of Saint Mary (see figs. 2.93, 2.94);
- Another frontal, a piece of Brussels rosepoint lace, was brought from Belgium in 1875. In 1952, Alice Wells, an Associate, gave the lace to the Community. It is used on Christmas, Easter, Transfiguration Day, and Profession days;
- A simple, crocheted frontal, made in 1958 by Mary Lillian Plowe, a former Bethany Home girl, is used for ferial days, when no feast is observed. It was restored by Sister Ursula Elizabeth in 1980.

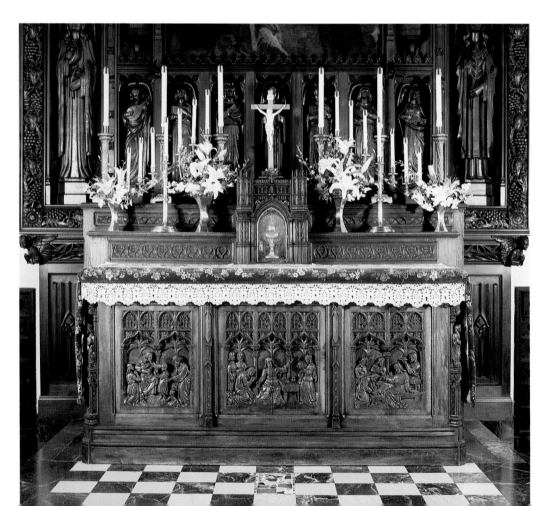

Fig. 2.94
Venetian Lace Frontal
with Velvet Altar Cover

Fig. 2.95
Chalices

Fig. 2.96
Eucharistic Vessels and Items
(clockwise from left rear) chalice, two silver
cruets, lavabo bowl, breadbox, and paten

LITURGICAL ITEMS
There are four chalices:

- A simple, silver Orthodox chalice, a gift of Sister Elizabeth of the Community of the Love of God, Kerala, India in 1995 (see fig. 2.95, left);
- A silver chalice with gold lining and jade knop, given by Sister Marjorie Hope in memory of her father (see fig. 2.95, center);
- A jeweled, gold-lined chalice, given in honor of Sister Katherine Helen. On the base is an opal whose rainbow radiance symbolizes hope. The base bears a cross of pearls, and the knop displays a sapphire. This extremely beautiful, unusual chalice is used for Christmas, Easter, Transfiguration Day, and other special liturgical celebrations (see fig. 2.95, right).
- A silver one, which has been used regularly since 1906, with scenes from the life of Jesus embossed on the base (see fig. 2.96);

Other Eucharistic vessels and items include two silver cruets, a lavabo bowl, an embossed silver breadbox, and paten (see fig. 2.96). There is also a second lavabo bowl; three abalone shells, carved in the Holy Land; a Gospel Book with brass cover; and small silver thurible.

WORKS OF ART
The priests' sacristy displays several notable pieces of art.

On the wall above the chest of drawers hangs a 15 in. x 30 in. ceramic crucifix by Anton Lang (1875-1938), a German studio potter (see fig. 2.97). The white corpus of the suffering Christ contrasts with the brown cross, which is draped with a wreath of green grape vines. Born in Oberammergau, Germany, Lang learned the potter's trade from his father. He played Jesus Christ in the Passion Play at Oberammergau in 1900, 1910, and 1922 (Lang 1930, 103).

Below the south window is a piscina, a sink used exclusively for cleansing ecclesiastical vessels and linens. It has no plumbing except for a drain that empties directly onto the earth. A 15-inch gilt ceramic Madonna stands on the windowsill above (see fig. 2.98). It is Ardalt Artware, handpainted in Japan.

Fig. 2.97
Crucifix
by Anton Lang
Ceramic. 15 in. x 30 in.

Fig. 2.98
Madonna
Ceramic. 16 ½ in. (height)

A wooden processional cross with a carved "Christus Rex" is kept in the northwest corner along with the processional torches; it is used during Holy Week (see fig. 2.99). The carver is unknown. Also in the sacristy is a large wooden crucifix that was carved by Fritz Abplanalp (see fig. 2.100). Placed on the altar from Maundy Thursday through Holy Saturday, it is used in the "Veneration of the Cross" devotion on Good Friday.

Above the desk is an ink drawing by Allen Rohan Crite (b.1910) (see fig. 2.101). In *The Eucharist*, a priest in Eucharistic vestments stands before a high altar, which is prepared for the celebration. Oversized altar candles and a crucifix of the suffering Christ tower above the altar. The chalice is hidden within the light created by the Presence. Below are the hand-printed words: "Who made there (by his one oblation of himself once offered) a full, perfect, and sufficient sacrifice, oblation, and satisfaction for the sins of the whole world."

On three walls hang copies of six etchings of Greek Fathers of the Church: Saints Cyril, Basil, Nicholas, John Chrysostom, Gregory Nazianzus, and Athanasius (see fig. 2.102). The artist is Francesco Bartolozzi (1727-1815), an Italian engraver who was preeminent in the art of stipple engraving.

The priests' sacristy formerly housed *The Missal*, illuminated by Sister Margaret Delores and bearing a leather cover, tooled by Sister Clara Elizabeth and inset with pearls. This magnificent work of art is now on display in the Convent library, having been superseded by the adoption of the 1979 *The Book of Common Prayer*.

The Working Sacristy

The working sacristy, immediately adjoining the priests' sacristy, is busy and well-used, providing space for a variety of housekeeping tools, cleaning supplies, candles, candelabras, flower vases, the thurible with its supply of incense, cabinets for storage of music and books, and a posting location for assigned Chapel duties, in addition to other relevant items and activities.

A framed poem, "Church Laundry," written by Sister Faith Marguerite and illuminated by another Sister, hangs on the wall above the sink (see fig. 2.103). On the west wall is a small wooden crucifix surrounded by the Stations of the Cross, embossed on brass (see fig. 2.104). On the south wall hangs a painting of the Virgin Mary by Sister Margaret Delores (see fig. 2.105).

Fig. 2.99
Processional Cross
Crucifix – wooden. 14 in. x 21½ in.
Pole – brass. 60 in.

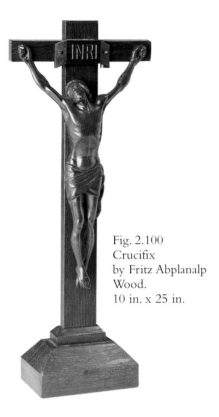

Fig. 2.100
Crucifix
by Fritz Abplanalp
Wood.
10 in. x 25 in.

Fig. 2.101
The Eucharist
by Allen Rohan Crite
Print. 3 3/8 in. x 5 3/4 in.

Fig. 2.102
Greek Father of the Church
by Francesco Bartolozzi
Etching (copy). 6 in. x 11 in.

Fig. 2.103
"Church Laundry"
Poem by Sister Faith Marguerite
Print (original). 9 3/4 in. x 15 3/4 in.

Fig. 2.104
Crucifix with Stations of the Cross
Wood and brass. 6 in. x 7 3/4 in.

Fig. 2.105
Virgin Mary
by Sister Margaret Delores
Painting (original). 15 1/2 in. x 20 in.

The bell tower is the north arm of the cruciform Chapel. The cornerstone of the Chapel is in its northeast corner, and in its west-facing wall is a statue of the Good Shepherd. It houses Saint Francis Chapel, the carillon, organ pipes, and stairwell. The north door of the bell tower leads straight ahead to the nave; to the left, it leads to Saint Francis Chapel.

Saint Francis Chapel

This small side chapel was originally known as the Children's Chapel or Children's Corner, and it was intended for the private devotions of Bethany Home children (see fig. 2.106). It is now dedicated to Saint Francis of Assisi (1181-1226), one of the most popular of all saints. Saint Francis is admired for his love and care of all creation, as well as for his identification with the poverty and suffering of Christ. In 1210, with the sanction of Pope Innocent III, he founded the Order of Friars Minor.

In 1916, Sister Clara Elizabeth and some of the Bethany Home girl students carved the altar of this chapel, beautifully and intricately marked with the Christmas rose, symbolizing the Nativity, and twining grapevine, symbolizing Christian unity and fruitfulness (see fig. 2.107). The altar was used originally in the former Convent's private oratory.

Unlike side chapels in many churches, the Saint Francis Chapel does not regularly house the Reserved Sacrament. However, during Holy Week, the Saint Francis Chapel altar becomes the "Altar of Repose." On Maundy Thursday, the reserved Sacrament is taken in a monstrance from the altar in the main Chapel to the Saint Francis Chapel altar, where the Community keeps vigil before it until noon of Good Friday.

Sister Clara Elizabeth carved the two wooden prie-dieus in front of the altar. An unfinished walnut statue of the Good Shepherd, carved by Fritz Abplanalp, stands on a small table to the right of the altar (see fig. 2.108).

Fig. 2.108
Good Shepherd (unfinished)
by Fritz Abplanalp
Wood. 26 in. (height)

Fig. 2.106
Saint Francis Chapel
9 ft. x 15 ft.

Fig. 2.107
Altar – Saint Francis Chapel
Wood. 36 in. (height)
Mensa 22 in. x 48 in.

Fig. 2.109
"Canticle of the Sun" Window
behind Saint Francis Chapel altar
dedicated June 11, 1929
20 in. x 47 in.

Fig. 2.110
St. Clare Window
in Bell Tower passage to nave
dedicated in 1960
20 in. x 47 in.

Behind and above the altar is the "Canticle of the Sun" window, the oldest stained glass window in the entire Chapel (see fig. 2.109). It depicts Jesus as a youth, surrounded by Mother Earth with the elements from "Canticle of the Sun": Brothers Wind, Sun and Fire, and Sisters Moon and Water. In the lower right corner, a Bethany Home girl sports the customary red-lined blue cape worn by the children in the 1920s. There are also some birds and animals. The base reads: "All thy works praise thee O Lord." Connick Studios designed the window, with suggestions from the Reverend Gilbert P. Symons, rector of Christ Church, Glendale, and brother of organist John Prower Symons. This window was dedicated during the hour just before the Chapel Service of Consecration on June 11, 1929.

The Saint Clare window was the last window installed; it is in the west wall of the passageway leading into the nave. It faces the "Canticle of the Sun" window, its counterpart (see fig. 2.110). This Connick glass window was installed in 1960, the last stained glass window to be added to the Chapel.

Saint Clare (1194-1253), the companion of Saint Francis, committed her life to following Christ's teachings. She and several other women formed the Order of the Poor Ladies of Saint Damiano at Assisi. They followed the Franciscan Rule and performed works of mercy for the poor and neglected. Clare herself was a servant, not only to the poor but also to her sisters. In the window she is dressed as an abbess, wearing a cincture with the three knots of poverty, chastity, and obedience and holding a crucifix. Above is a monstrance and below are the words: "Have no fear little daughters trust in Jesus."

A foot-high, marble-like figurine of Saint Francis with animals perches on the windowsill, a copy of the original sculpture by G. Ruggeri (see fig. 2.111).

Sister Margaret Delores illuminated and printed in calligraphy the framed copy of "The Canticle of the Sun," which hangs on the north side of the passageway into the Saint Francis Chapel (see fig. 2.112). Saint Francis composed "Canticle of the Sun," which reveals his spirit of joyous faith and love for all creatures, while at St. Clare's convent of Saint Damiano in Assisi, Italy. On the south side is an icon of Saint Francis (see fig. 2.113). The artist is unknown.

Fig. 2.111
Saint Francis Statue
by G. Ruggeri
Copy. 12 in. (height)

Fig. 2.113
Saint Francis
Icon. 10 in. x 17 in.

Fig. 2.112
"The Canticle of the Sun"
illuminated by Sister Margaret Delores
11 in. x 13 3/4 in.

Fig. 2.114
Jesus with Little Children
by Margaret W. Tarrant
Print. 15 in. x 21 in.

On the south wall hangs a picture of Jesus with little children, painted by Margaret W. Tarrant (see fig. 2.114). Jesus is holding a little girl and her doll against His right shoulder. Children surround and look up to Him, and His left hand is stretched out to bless a little girl. A blue background arches over the composition. In the two upper corners, young angels oversee them. In the border are the words: "Suffer Little Children to Come Unto Me."

The Stations of the Cross in Saint Francis Chapel are several hundred years old (see fig. 2.115). Jane (Mrs. Horace) Gray, sister of Mother Eva, purchased them at a private auction of furnishings from the chapel of a dismantled French chateau. The scenes of the Stations are medieval in design. For example, they portray soldiers in chain mail armor.

Of dark blue enamel with touches of gold, the Stations are Limoges porcelain, generally considered to be the finest enamelware produced in Europe in the sixteenth and seventeenth centuries. To produce these works of art, which are painted enameled copper, the metal was slightly domed with a burnisher, then coated equally over the entire surface with dark blue enamel and fired. Coats of white enamel in varying thicknesses were then applied, and the design was executed with a needle or stylus. After the final refiring, touches of gold were added to enhance the design.

On the wall to the right of the Saint Clare window is a list of the carillon's thirty-six bells, indicating the weight and name of each bell, and the note the bell plays (see fig. 2.116). Sister Clara Elizabeth did the illumination and calligraphy.

In the north wall of Saint Francis Chapel, there are four doors. The first door on the left leads downstairs to the undercroft. The next two doors are for the confessional, which is rarely used since the building of the present Convent with a confessional in the oratory. The fourth door leads to stairs that reach up to the organ chamber. From this landing, a ladder reaches the clavier room and carillon.

Fig. 2.115
Station of the Cross
Limoges porcelain. 8 in. x 8 in.

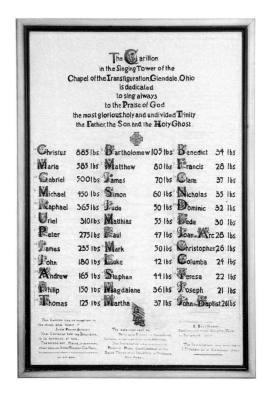

Fig. 2.116
List of Carillon Bells
by Sister Clara Elizabeth
north transept, west wall
Original. 26 in. x 38 in.

Fig. 2.117
Carillon Bells

Carillon

The Sisters originally planned to install a peal of bells in the Chapel bell tower, but changed those plans to include a carillon of two octaves, thanks to John Prower Symons (1870-1937). Symons presented the idea for a Chapel carillon to the Sisters in the late 1920s (see fig. 2.117). Further, he agreed to find enough money to enable the Community to enlarge the scope of the project (Breiel 1934, 9).

Fig. 2.118
Clavier in Bell Tower

Fig. 2.119
Sister Ruth Magdalene
(1883-1973)
Missionary, intercessor, musician,
teacher, writer, carillonneur

It is easy to see why Symons was so committed to the Chapel carillon project. Former head of the music department of Thiel College in Greenville, Pennsylvania, Symons had first become associated with the Sisters and the children of Bethany Home by giving organ, piano, and voice lessons there. He often played the organ for Chapel services, and instructed the children in music for special occasions. An accomplished carillonneur, Symons attended the first Congress of the Guild of Carillonneurs in North America (GCNA) in 1934 and was an early member of that organization, according to his nephew Gilbert Symons. Symons also served as a consultant for the Van Duzen Bell Foundry, Cincinnati, Ohio.

The carillon was a lifelong passion for Symons. According to an article in the *Cincinnati Post*, Symons "became interested in bell music when he was a boy in England…[and] learned to love the bells of [the many churches in] his community…. Mr. Symons traveled to Belgium and Holland, where he studied the carillons, went to school, and became one of the world's leading carilloneurs." (Breiel 1934, 9) Symons studied under one of the foremost carilloneurs, Josef Denyn, founder of the carillon school in Mechlin, Belgium.

A carillon is much more complex than a peal of bells, in which bells of various notes are rung in succession to create simple melodies. The carillon, instead, is a musical instrument "of at least two octaves of fixed, cup-shaped bells arranged in chromatic series and so tuned as to produce, when many such bells are sounded together, concordant harmony." (Bigelow 1984, 4) The carillonneur plays the instrument from a clavier or keyboard, which controls expression through variation of touch (see fig. 2.118).

After Symon's considerable fundraising, research, hard work, and experimentation with design, Van Duzen Foundry cast and installed a twenty-five-bell carillon in the bell tower under his direction. The Denyn method was used to connect the bells to the clavier.

The November, 1931 issue of *The Bethany Home Chronicle*, a monthly publication by Bethany Home girls, reports: "There was great excitement as we watched 25 bells swing high into our Chapel tower. We are all eagerly waiting to hear our carillon play for the first time. The two octaves of 25 bells were hung high in the Chapel's bell tower, bolted in place on wooden beams. The clavier was placed below near the Children's Chapel."

The carillon rang out its songs for a while, but then was silent for years. In the winter, 1949 *Transfiguration Quarterly*, the Community bulletin, Sister Ruth Magdalene, organist and carillonneur (see fig. 2.119), reported:

> Many of our readers know that there is a carillon in our Chapel tower. It was installed at the time the Chapel was built, and for a while we used the bells but it did not take long for us to realize that they were not in good tune and ever since we have been hoping that the day would come when we could have them reconditioned…. However, there would be no bells in our tower had it not been for the love and desire of our dear friend Mr. John Prower Symons.
>
> Three weeks ago, Mr. Boyd Jordan, the carillonneur of the singing tower at Mariemont, [Ohio,] brought over here a young Hollander, Mr. Fritsen, who represented the firm of Petit and Fritsen. [This company has] been making bells in the low countries of Europe for nearly three hundred years. Mr. Fritsen had been sent to see our bells by Mr. Price, the carillonneur of the Charles Baird carillon at Ann Arbor, Michigan. He had seen the bells and heard them last year and he was interested in doing what he could to help us. Mr. Fritsen told us that his firm had made several single bells for our country but they have no carillon over here. And they are so anxious to make a carillon for some place in the United States that they have made us a very amazing offer which we are advised to accept (Ruth 1949, 12-13).

By 1949, there were enough funds to send the entire Symons set of bells, with an order for one more, to Petit and Fritsen in Aarel-Rixtel, Holland for recasting. Mr. Fritsen designed the re-castings. Sister Ruth reported in the summer, 1950 *Quarterly* that "each bell was to be inscribed with the Jerusalem Cross and the letters 'AMDG' for 'Ad Maiorem Dei Gloriam': To the Greater Glory of God.... The biggest bell, named Christus, A# below middle C, will weigh 885 pounds and its diameter will be 2 feet and 10 inches. As bells go, this is not very large but for the present it is our bourdon. By way of contrast our smallest bell, named John Baptist, A#, two octaves above middle C, will weigh 20 pounds and its diameter will be 7 inches." (Ruth 1950, 16)

The bells were re-cast and shipped from Holland to Ohio. In the autumn, 1950 *Quarterly*, Sister Ruth wrote: "They are here! They arrived in Glendale the first day of August, and it was an exciting moment for me when I peered into the truck and had my first glimpse of our beautiful bells! And they are beautiful – the one in memory of dear Mother Eva Mary has special decorations on it, but all of them are things of beauty and, as I sounded each one, dangling in the air as they were unloaded, the tone was all that I had hoped for." (Ruth 1950, 18-19) (see fig. 2.120)

The bells were blessed on the afternoon of August 2, 1950 (see fig. 2.121). Then, before those bells were installed, ten more were ordered to bring the instrument up to three full octaves. The twenty-six bells, arranged in order of size, remained on planks that rested on cement blocks at the north side of the Chapel until the final ten arrived. The I. T. Verdin Company, Cincinnati, Ohio, executed the installation of the bells from drawings made by Percival Price, a prominent carillonneur and composer of carillon music noted for his expert knowledge of carillon installation.

Sister Ruth Magdalene was the first to play the new carillon. She wrote in the summer, 1951 *Quarterly*: "It is considered by those who know to be a very fine piece of work. The frame is of steel, but the bells all hang on great wooden beams, which makes the tone sweeter and softer. The countless rods and wires connect the beautiful bells with the clavier and the action is easier than that of a piano."(Ruth 1951, 8)

Fig. 2.121
Blessing of the Bells

Fig. 2.120
Carillon Bells – detail

Fig. 2.122
Carillon Renovation

Fig. 2.123
Albert Meyer Playing Carillon

On Trinity Sunday, May 20, 1951, Percival Price played the dedication recital of the bells. It was a glorious day and hundreds of people came to hear the music. Sister Ruth wrote:

> Mr. Price is one of our foremost carillonneurs and under his skilled touch the bells sang and rippled and shouted for joy. It was a joyous occasion. He began with the glorious old hymn tune 'Holy, Holy, Holy,' of course one of the special hymns for Trinity Sunday. He played it first on the upper bells very simply and then the second and third times more and more of the bells rang out in happy variations until all the Apostles and other saints for whom the bells are named were taking their part.... We really had never heard the bells do their very best before. Mendelssohn's 'Spring Song' was very lovely as it floated down from the tower and 'Jesu, Joy of Man's Desiring' showed how the music of bells lends itself to such classic compositions. (Ruth 1951, 8)

At Mr. Price's suggestion, a little cabin of brown wallboard with insulation was built around the keyboard in the tower. In the *Quarterly* of winter, 1951, Sister Ruth reported: "The well, coming up through the organ chamber forests of pipes, yields just enough inches for the upward thrust of the three ladders leading to the bell deck. It has been ingeniously covered at the top and from it you step into the clavier room." (Ruth 1951, 11)

Soon, melodious carillon music once again floated across the village of Glendale, a sound welcomed by the Community and its neighbors alike.

Forty years later, having been played thousands of times in all temperatures and conditions of humidity, the carillon was in need of repair. The renovation of the organ chambers in the 1980s provided space to create easier access to the clavier cabin. In 1991, the Verdin Company renovated the carillon. At that time, carillonneur Richard Watson designed and installed a new clavier with an enlarged pedal-board of one and a half octaves, and the original clavier was relocated to the Verdin Company's Bell Museum in Cincinnati's Over-the-Rhine. As part of this renovation, Watson moved and rehung some of the bells and designed a completely new transmission action, using sealed ball bearings. Because the clappers were striking the sound bow at the wrong point and many of the clapper weights were not optimum, Watson designed new clappers for every bell. The striking ball of each new clapper is made from a special cast iron alloy, which brings forth a warm, mellow, well-balanced tone from each bell (see fig. 2.122).

The carillon was rededicated on Transfiguration Day, August 6, 1991. Albert Meyer, carillonneur at the Emery Memorial Carillon in Mariemont, a village east of Cincinnati, played some of the music from the original dedicatory recital. He also included other music, written especially for this instrument. Sister Ruth Magdalene had arranged some of those pieces.

Sister Ruth Magdalene (1883–1973) joyously played the carillon as long as her health permitted. Several other Sisters have played it, in particular Sister Monica Mary, as well as the Reverend Ralph Spinner, one of the former Convent chaplains. Since 1962, Albert Meyer has played a carillon recital almost every Monday evening (see fig. 2.123).

At the invitation of the Community, the Congress of the Guild of Carillonneurs of North America met at the Convent in Glendale three times: in 1952, 1974, and 1992.

The Campanologists

(Time Magazine, July 7, 1952)

In Mariemont, Ohio one day last week, Mayor E. Boyd Jordan mounted the 100-ft. tower of the town carillon and entered the tiny clavier room. He loosened his collar and tie, rolled up his sleeves. He rubbed his arms and hands with alcohol, fastened leather guards over his hands, sat down at the keyboard and started pummeling its projecting levers, stamping on its pedals. Above him in the belfry, 23 tuned bells chimed out a program of folk tunes, hymns, a classical number or two. The annual congress of the Guild of Carillonneurs of North America was in town, and Host Carillonneur Jordan was playing them a welcoming recital.

Why should carillonneurs hold a convention? Campanology is a lonely profession. The performer sits in his enclosed cubicle and may pound until he pants, but he rarely hears much more than a jumble of overtones, mixed with the clatter of the levers. Moreover, there are only 79 carillons in North America (eight of them in Canada), so performers rarely have a chance to compare notes. In Mariemont, a suburb of Cincinnati, guildmen wasted only an hour on formalities, got down to business in a hurry: for the better part of three days they took turns at keyboards in the vicinity while the rest lounged listening outside....

Mayor Jordan took members to nearby Glendale where members played on the 36-bell carillon of the Episcopal Sisters of the Transfiguration. His proudest moment came when his pupil, Sister Ruth Magdalene, a onetime missionary in China who has studied for only one year, put on the leather guards, pulled up her skirts a bit so that her feet could be freer for the heavy pedals, and rang out a pair of selections. Sister Ruth Magdalene was promptly voted into the guild.

Ring those bells!

A rope attached to the Christus bell descends into the northeast corner of the choir. It is used to ring the bell to signal the beginning of the Eucharist and other services and to ring the Angelus.

A swinging bell is also located in the bell tower, and a rope descends from it into Saint Francis Chapel. This bell is rung to announce the time for daily Evensong and Sunday Eucharist.

UNDERCROFT

The Chapel undercroft, reached via a door in Saint Francis Chapel's north wall, consists of two rooms. The larger was intended for use as the chapter room, the area where the Community holds meetings of the governing body of professed members. A chapter room is an important center in a religious community, and this undercroft room served the purpose for many years.

When Mother Eva and Sister Beatrice visited convents in England, they saw chapter rooms that included carved stalls with parapets surrounding a council table. Using these as a model, the Sisters decided upon a similar, but more simple, arrangement for the chapter room of the Community of the Transfiguration.

Since the present Convent was completed in 1970, chapter meetings have been held in the Convent because it became too difficult for some Sisters to access this room, particularly in inclement weather. In 1979, the chapter room was refurnished as a religious education classroom for Bethany School.

The table that now graces the room first was used as a temporary altar over the casket at Mother Eva's requiem. Then, with its legs shortened, it became the council table. Since then, the council table has taken on a different function: the ironing board for ecclesiastical linens.

The other room in the undercroft served first as a studio for woodcarver Fritz Abplanalp in the 1930s. Since then, it has been used as a storage room. Among the contents are two creche sets used from Christmas Eve through Christmastide. One set, a miniature log stable (24 in. x 40 in.) with creamy-white ceramic figurines, is placed in the northwest corner of the nave. The other, a wooden stable (14 in. x 18 in.) with white, marble-like painted figurines made of plaster of Paris, is placed to the left of the altar in Saint Francis Chapel.

Fig. 2.125
Sister Helen Veronica (1889-1976)
Spiritual director, missionary, gardener, foundress of Chinese Community of the Transfiguration

CHAPEL GARDENS

Just as the Chapel of the Transfiguration is a place of tranquility and beauty in every season of the year, so are the Virgin's Garden and cutting garden that adjoin it.

The Virgin's Garden graces the south side of the Chapel (see fig. 2.124). This beloved garden had its beginning in the early 1930s as the inspiration and work of Sister Helen Veronica (see fig. 2.125). She planned the Virgin's Garden to be clearly viewed from the north door through the south door. As a result, the view from inside the Chapel is one of an arched doorway, framing a graceful Carrara marble statue of Saint Mary with the Child Jesus.

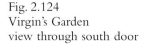

Fig. 2.124
Virgin's Garden
view through south door

Fig. 2.126
Statue of Saint Mary with the Child Jesus

This sensitive representation of Mother and Child is situated in the center of the south border of the garden, comprised of rose and boxwood bushes (see fig. 2.126). Tall deciduous and evergreen trees provide a soft, textured background for the statue. Mary holds her Child against her left shoulder. Looking down at Him with a mother's attitude of humility and compassion, she contemplates the Child with awe while He, cradled in her arms, looks up to her. Due to deterioration by weather, the first statue of Mary and the Child Jesus was replaced with the present one, which was imported from Italy.

From the south door, a steppingstone walk leads garden visitors through a quiet, inviting rock garden where a variety of colorful ground covers fill the area (see fig. 2.127). Evergreen trees provide shade all day long. The walk opens onto a lawn where benches are provided and to a border in front of the statue, where, in season, spring bulbs and summer annuals contribute a rainbow of flowers in constant bloom.

Caretakers for the Virgin's Garden have included Sisters Mary Agnes, Mary Catherine, Grace Elizabeth, Helena Miriam, and Louise Magdalene. Sister Grace Elizabeth added the cutting garden to enable enjoyment of the flowers both indoors and out (see fig. 2.128). Since 1990, a young woman who lives on the Convent grounds has tended both gardens.

These gardens have served the Community and its guests well as sought-after places of beauty, respite, meditation, and celebration. In years gone by, Bethany Home girls celebrated May Day here, and at other times they held drama and musical performances. Today it is a place set apart for Sisters, retreatants, and guests.

Beautiful flowers from the cutting garden adorn Community altars, add a greeting of hospitality to the dining areas and guest rooms, and become thoughtful gifts for families and friends.

Fig. 2.127
Rock Garden

Fig. 2.128
Cutting Garden

GIFTS AND MEMORIALS

All your works shall give thanks to you,

O Lord, and all your faithful shall bless you.

(Psalm 145:10)

ver since it was only a dream in the heart of Mother Foundress Eva Mary, the Community of the Transfiguration has received many generous gifts and memorials for the Chapel of the Transfiguration from countless friends, Bethany Home children, Associates, and Sisters, as well as the family of Mother Eva. Whatever the gift, all have been received with gratitude and appreciation. The memories and prayers of those who have worshiped and continue to worship in the Chapel have made it truly a special place where God is glorified.

 The Chapel might indeed be considered a memorial to Sister Beatrice Martha, who so perfectly and completely fulfilled Mother Eva's dream. It was Sister Beatrice who was responsible for the planning and building of the Chapel, as well as supervision of the furnishings and decorations of the Chapel until her death in 1963. Sister Beatrice was remarkably successful in carrying out her "commission."

 In a spirit of thanksgiving, the Community has attempted to cite below the many gifts and memorials made on behalf of the Chapel in the past hundred years. Every attempt has been made for accuracy and completeness, but it is possible that some gifts and memorials may have been omitted inadvertently. If this is the case, the Community expresses its most sincere apologies and would appreciate appropriate information.

 Items are listed by Chapel location, then chronologically, except for those items given prior to 1929 (listed under "Transition Items") and all windows (listed under "Windows").

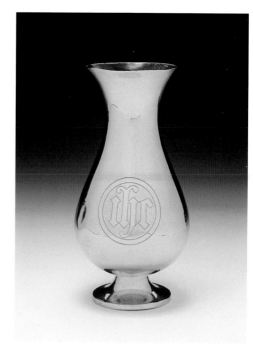

Figure 3.1
Altar Vase
8 in. (height)

Transition Items

The following items were moved from the former Convent chapel or oratory to the new Chapel of the Transfiguration in 1929.

- Set of brass altar vases – in memory of Harold Baker Aull (c.1900) (see fig. 3.1)

- Baptismal font – a memorial to Mother Eva Mary's niece, Baby Faith Cleveland, who died at birth and was baptized by her faithful Roman Catholic nurse (1900)

- Brass processional cross – in memory of Luella Heff (1901)

- Pascal candle stand – in memory of Sister Ellis Victoria (1906)

- Silver chalice, embossed with the life of Jesus – in memory of Louise Sampson (1906)

- *Singing Cherubs* frieze (copy) – in memory of Augusta B. Henderson, Sister Beatrice's mother (1907). Mrs. Henderson taught the children singing and was the Community's first Associate. She assisted in the work of Bethany Home from the beginning until her death in 1907. "She lived with the Sisters and gave herself generously to the work with little children calling herself shyly, 'the Mother Inferior.'" (Cleveland 1929, 128)

- Set of six etchings of Greek Fathers – gift from Jane (Mrs. Horace) Gray, sister of Mother Eva (c.1920)

Figure 3.2
Altar Vase
8 in. (height)

Fig. 3.3
Monstrance

In the Nave

- *Madonna in Adoration* bas-relief sculpture (copy) – gift from Dr. Ralph Adams Cram, Chapel architect (1928)

- *St. Michael and the Dragon* statue – given by two Associates, sisters Florence and Laura Roberts, of Trenton, New Jersey, following their first retreat at the Community (1930)

- *The Transfiguration*, an icon painted on a rock from Mt. Tabor – a gift from the Russian Orthodox Sisters (c.1940)

- *A Group of Saints*, an original painting by Miguel Cabrera, has been in the Sisters' custody since 1951. Mr. Chew, an art collector from Xenia, Ohio, offered the painting as a gift to the Diocese of Southern Ohio. Mr. Chew had started a collection of portraits and needed space for his new acquisitions. Bishop Henry Hobson suggested that it might be placed in the Chapel of the Transfiguration "on loan," and it has remained there ever since.

In the Choir

- Rood screen – in memory of Harlan Cleveland, Society trustee and first business advisor, by his wife Grace, Mother Eva's sister (1929)

- Möller organ – given by Mrs. Cooper Procter in honor of her sister, Mary H. Johnston, who was the first singing teacher at Bethany Home (1929)

- Four choir lights – memorials to Sisters Ada Frances, Frances Mabel, Mary Joseph, and Emily Faith; the latter had met the Sisters when she was a missionary in China. (1929)

- Theotokos Hodigitria icon – gift from Bishop Boyd Vincent; it had belonged to his sister (c.1930)

- Christus Pantocrator icon – given by Associate Mrs. A.J. Alexander of Columbus, Ohio (1960)

- The Bible (Revised Standard Version) on the ambo – gift from Saint John's Home in Painesville, Ohio (Christmas, 1973)

- As a free-will offering of thanksgiving for the Sisters' hospitality to him and his family, Robert Maye of Akron, Ohio, gave his talent and time in working on the Schantz organ. This included tuning, taking out and returning the great division during ceiling repairs, adding the four-bell cymbalstern, and softening the great division. (October, 1983)

In the Sanctuary

- Three sanctuary lights – given by the Associates as a memorial for Mother Eva (1929)

- Altar rail – in memory of the Reverend Stanley Matthews Cleveland (1889-1926), a Convent chaplain, by his mother, Grace (Mrs. Harlan) Cleveland, sister of Mother Eva (1929)

- Reredos – given by the Community in memory of Mortimer Matthews, Mother Eva's brother (1929). Society trustee and the Community's first legal advisor, he was also the father of Sister Olivia Mary and Sister Mary Catherine.

- Eucharistic candlesticks – in memory of Miss Kate Steineman by her niece, Sister Lillian Martha (1950)

In the Sacristies

- Processional torches – in memory of Elizabeth Waterman, Sister Joanna Mary's mother (1929)

- Small brass crucifix with embossed Stations of the Cross – given by the Reverend Charles Lea on the day of the Service of Consecration of the Chapel, June 11, 1929. In Sister Beatrice's letter about the service, she states that Father Lea was chief thurifer.

- Blue velvet altar cover – a gift from Sister Alexis of the Russian Orthodox Church (c.1929)

- Set of brass altar vases – in memory of Marjorie Montmorency, who helped with the Bethany Home children from the beginning until her death (1943) (see figure 3.2)

- Rosewood monstrance – given by the Reverend Paul Thompson (late 1980s) (see fig. 3.3)

- Belgian rosepoint lace – brought from Brussels in 1875 and given by Associate Alice Wells (1952)

- The "Holy Family," a set of twelve-inch ceramic figurines – made and given by Mother Meribal, CSMV, Wantage, England (1930) (see figs. 3.4, 3.5)

- Silver chalice with gold lining and jade knop – given by Sister Marjorie Hope in memory of her father, Charles Harkness (1965)

- Two silver cruets – in memory of Sister Deborah Ruth (1972)

- Jeweled chalice – in honor of Sister Katherine Helen (1974)

- Altar book – given by Sister Dorothea Mary on the fiftieth anniversary of her profession (October 4, 1981)

- Gospel book – in memory of Lorraine Barnes, an Associate who was received in 1950 and died in 1982 (c.1982)

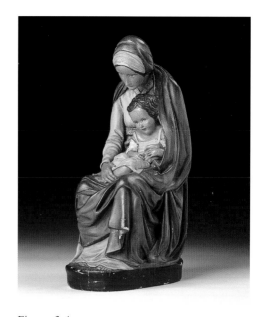

Figure 3.4
Madonna and Child (Holy Family set)
12 in. (height)

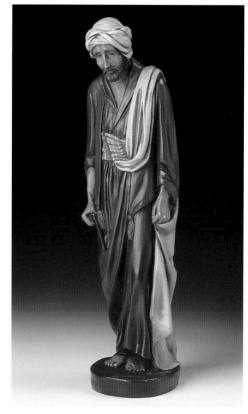

Figure 3.5
Joseph (Holy Family set)
17 in. (height)

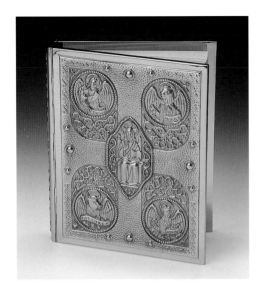

Fig. 3.6
Gospel Book

Fig. 3.7
Altar Vase
4 in. x 11 in.

- Two fair linens – made for the altar in Saint Luke's House, Lincolnton, North Carolina and now used on the Saint Francis Chapel altar; handwoven and given by Associate Lillie Wood of Kansas (1989)

- Gospel book with a brass cover – given by Bishop John Allin when he was the Community's Chaplain General from 1986-1991 (1990) (see fig. 3.6)

- Set of white vestments with coronation tapestry orphreys – given by Sister Jean Gabriel in memory of her parents, Ralph and Ethel Crothers (1992)

- Silver Orthodox chalice and small silver thurible – gift from Sister Elizabeth of the Community of the Love of God, Kerala, India (1995)

- Set of rectangular brass altar vases – in memory of Mary Lillian, Mildred Anne, and Margaret Louise Plowe and Mrs. Gwendoline Roemler by their friends (1999). The Plowe triplets came to Bethany Home when they were seven years old, in the fall of 1929. Mrs. Roemler's mother was associated with Mother Eva when she ministered in Omaha, Nebraska; Gwen was received as an Associate in 1937 and died in 1998. (see fig. 3.7)

In the Bell Tower

- Set of small brass candlesticks – in memory of Adaline Dunbar (1945). These are on the altar in Saint Francis Chapel.

- Figurine of Saint Francis in Saint Francis Chapel – gift from the Reverend Raymond Sturm (1990)

- Icon of Saint Francis – brought by Sister Althea Augustine from Assisi (1990)

- Renovation of the carillon and installation of a new clavier – given by Sister Margaret Alice in memory of her father, John Gerald Allen (1991)

- Carillon bells (1931-49)
    - Christus – in memory of John Prower Symons
    - Maria – in memory of Mother Eva Mary
    - Gabriel – in memory of Mrs. Margaret Hester, mother of Sister Mariya Margaret
    - Michael – in memory of Mrs. Jane Gray, sister of Mother Eva
    - Raphael – in memory of Anne, a Bethany Home girl
    - Uriel – in memory of Jeanie, a Bethany Home girl
    - Peter and Francis – in memory of boys and girls of Bethany Home
    - James – in memory of Emily B. Carruthers
    - John – in memory of Charles, John, and Edward, Bethany Home boys
    - Andrew – in memory of W.A. Sayers
    - Philip – given by Mrs. Granville in memory of her mother and brothers
    - James, Mark, and Stephen – given by Mrs. Alice West Shell in memory of Albert A. Shell
    - Magdalene – in memory of H.B. Podmore
    - Martha and Benedict – in memory of the Associates
    - John Baptist – in memory of the Reverend Gilbert P. Symons

Windows

- "Canticle of the Sun" window – the first window installed. Given by Jane (Mrs. Horace) Gray, Mother Eva's sister, possibly as a memorial to Mother Eva (1929); dedicated on June 11, 1929

- Mother Eva Mary window – given by Bethany Home boys and girls; dedicated on August 6, 1948

- Saint Boniface window – given by the Community in memory of Bishop Irving Johnson; dedicated on October 18, 1948

- Round window – given by Bishop Paul Matthews to commemorate the fifty-seventh anniversary of his and Bishop Irving Johnson's ordination to the priesthood; dedicated on October 18, 1948

- Virgin Mary window – given by the Community in memory of Grace Matthews (Mrs. Harlan) Cleveland; dedicated on March 25, 1949 (see fig. 3.8)

- Saint Bride and Saint Hilda windows – given by the Community as an expression of thanksgiving in honor of Bishop Matthews and Bishop Johnson; dedicated on March 25, 1949

- Saint Elizabeth window – given by the Community in memory of Grace Matthews (Mrs. Harlan) Cleveland; dedicated on June 11, 1952 (see fig. 3.9)

- Mother Harriet Monsell and John Mason Neale windows – given by the Community in honor of the wedding anniversary of Bishop and Mrs. Paul Matthews; dedicated on May 11, 1956

- Saint Lioba window – given by the Community in memory of Marianna Procter (Mrs. Mortimer) Matthews, sister-in-law of Mother Eva and mother of Sister Olivia Mary and Sister Mary Catherine. Sister Olivia Mary was Mother Superior at the time of dedication in 1959.

- Saint Clare window – the last window installed. Given by the Community in memory of Sister Clara Elizabeth; dedicated in 1960

Fig. 3.8
Virgin Mary Window – detail
Garden of Eden

Fig. 3.9
St. Elizabeth Window – detail
Zachariah with Angel

Mother Foundress Eva Mary, C.T.
(1862–1928)

"The nearer we are to God, the more full we are of joy."

— *Mother Foundress Eva Mary, C.T.*

As in the beginning and throughout the years, the Chapel continues to be the center of the life of the Community of the Transfiguration. Here the Sisters and many others worship together, offering praise, intercession, and thanksgiving to God, Who makes all things possible. May the vision of Mother Eva Mary and Sister Beatrice Martha and their devotion to the Mystery of the Transfiguration be carried on in days to come by all those who worship in this Chapel, and through the religious life and witness of their Sisters — lives of prayer and service, offered to the glory of God.

Work by the following artists is represented in the Chapel of the Transfiguration, either as originals or fine copies.

Bartolozzi, Francisco (1725-1815) – born in Florence, Italy. This Italian painter, designer, and engraver first worked as in the Venice shop of Joseph Wagner, an historical engraver and print-seller, then relocated to Rome in 1760. His appointment as engraver to George III brought him to London in 1764. Although his worldwide reputation had been that of a line engraver, Bartolozzi began exploring the new method of stipple engraving (commonly known as the "red chalk" style because of its reddish-brown ink printing), and turned it into an art. Thus he became known as "the master in stipple." His fellow engravers openly acknowledged the superiority of his work, and appeared to be content to learn from him. Bartolozzi's genius lay not only in the detail and delicate effects of his artistic prints, but also in his prolific production. Bartolozzi engraved portraits, Hogarth's drawings, Cipriani's designs, and fanciful subjects – whatever was commissioned. After moving to Lisbon in 1802 at the request of the Portuguese prince regent, he was named director of the National Academy at Lisbon and continued to work until his death. (Bartolozzi 1883, 115ff)

Cabrera, Miguel (1695-1786) – a Mexican Indian, born in Antequera (now Oaxaca), Mexico. Sometimes referred to as "the Murillo of New Spain," he was a prolific painter of mostly religious subjects and an excellent portrait artist. In 1754, he was among several painters who formed an academy of art in Mexico City. Much of Cabrera's work is inspired by older European artistic style, but he was also innovative in his exploration of group portraits that included individuals with marked ethnic differences, as shown clearly in *A Group of Saints*. (Turner 1996, 1:355; Meyers 1969, 453)

Crite, Allen Rohan (1910-) – born in North Plainfield, New Jersey; as a boy, moved with his parents to Roxbury, a section of Boston. Studied at Boston University, The Massachusetts College of Art, and Harvard University. Much of Crite's work emerged from his childhood experiences in Roxbury. He describes himself as an "artist reporter," whose oil paintings, lithographs, and ink drawings depict the joys and sorrows of everyday city neighborhood life. Crite has expressed acute sensitivity to stereotypes of African Americans, and in his religious art Crite attempts to convey the dignity and deep spirituality of African Americans. Crite always used his art to teach, whether for religious or historical reasons. He contributed to Boston's African American art scene by establishing the Artists' Collective, a forum for emerging African American artists. In 1968, he initiated a project for schoolchildren on the cultural heritage of the United States. Two of Crite's works are in the permanent collection of the Smithsonian's National Museum of American Art in Washington, D.C. (Strychasz 1998, online)

del Sarto, Andrea (1486-1530) – a Florentine painter of the High Renaissance. He started his career as an apprentice to a goldsmith, but eventually discovered his true talents, found the right teachers, and developed into one of the finest fresco painters of the time. It is suggested by some that his talents may even have equaled those of Raphael and Michelangelo. del Sarto was flexible in his use of technique, willing to take risks with traditional rules of coloring, and able to learn from others. He continued to learn and grow as an artist until his death from the plague at the age of 43. (*Encyclopedia Britannica*, 15th ed.)

della Robbia, Andrea – see **della Robbia, Luca**

della Robbia, Luca (c.1399-1482) – a sculptor and one of the pioneers of the Florentine Renaissance style. He was the founder of the della Robbia family studio primarily associated with the production of sculpture in enameled terra cotta. The della Robbia family distinguished themselves in Florence in the late fifteenth and sixteenth centuries, especially the sculptor Luca della Robbia and his nephew Andrea, for their exquisite works of bas and high relief sculptures. Besides statues in marble and bronze, Luca della Robbia is credited with perfecting a technique for producing glazed terra cotta reliefs. He used a glaze made white and opaque by the addition of tin oxide. Andrea would sometimes omit the application of the glaze on faces and hands if he had done particularly detailed and realistic work on them. The della Robbias were noted for reliefs in white against a blue background. Many were surrounded with wreaths of finely carved, brilliantly colored fruits, pine cones, or flowers. Their use of color is considered particularly outstanding. From the della Robbias came many reliefs of babies, cherubs, and Madonnas, among countless other works of religious art that adorn churches, hospitals, museums and other public institutions in many countries. The della Robbias' enameled terra cotta technique was imitated widely and spread throughout Europe; often the terra cotta was painted in natural colors or to imitate marble or bronze. (*New Columbia Encyclopedia*, 4th ed.; Domestici 1992, 58)

Lang, Anton (1875-1938) – a native of Oberammergau, Germany and potter by trade, Lang played the role of Christ in the Passion Play of 1900, 1910, and 1922. Requirements for participation in the Passion Play include being a native of Oberammergau, of high moral character, and dramatically qualified. In 1633, the Black Plague caused the death of many people in Oberammergau. The remaining villagers held a prayer service, at which time the epidemic ended there even though it continued to ravage the rest of Europe. As an expression of gratitude, villagers vowed to enact the passion and death of Jesus Christ every ten years, with the first performance given in 1634.

During the Depression, the 1920 production of the Passion Play was postponed to 1922. The proceeds from that production did not meet expenses so, with the help of some United States supporters, a U.S. tour of exhibits of Oberammergau "home art" was arranged. Lang and several other members of the cast made the trip in 1923. When in Cincinnati, he visited the Rookwood Pottery Company. Lang's pottery, marked with his name in script, is fairly scarce and highly valued for its artistic quality. (*Encyclopedia Britannica*, 14th ed.; Lang 1930, 115)

Murillo, Bartolome Estaben (1618-1682) – born in Seville, Spain. When quite young, Murillo was apprenticed to a painter, but when that teacher moved to another city, he was forced to make his own living painting rough religious art at public fairs. With the help of a patron, he studied, practiced, and copied in Italy for two years before returning to Spain. Murillo's technique softened and "warmed" over the years. He painted dozens of memorable religious works, many for the Franciscans, which reflect his own mysticism and piety, as well as the piety of the times. His few portraits are renowned for their beauty and realism, as are his many life-like paintings of the street children of Seville. Murillo died after a fall from scaffolding while painting. (*New Columbia Encyclopedia*, 4th ed.)

Raphael (1483-1520) – born Raffaelo Santi or Raffaello Sanzio in Urbino, Italy. His early training was from his father, painter Giovanni Santi. His paintings are exquisite and luminous, many of them icons in the sense of being windows through which one looks to see the truth beyond. Part of his brilliance comes from his attention to detail and his intense work studying the beauties and intricacies of the human form. Many of his works, frescoes, and paintings are in the Vatican. Raphael was also a preservationist. When Pope Julius II wanted Raphael to do new frescoes in several rooms of the Vatican whose walls were already covered with frescoes by masters, Raphael managed to save one room, and had his students copy a number of portrait heads from the others before they were destroyed. A sculptor, architect, and archeologist of note, Raphael died on his thirty-seventh birthday after a short illness. (*Encyclopedia Britannica*, 15th ed.)

Ribalta, Francisco (1565-1628) – born in Castellon, Spain and probably trained at the Escorial. A painter from the heart whose soft, gentle brushwork brings life and power to a variety of religious subjects, Ribalta's works reflect not only contemporary Spanish mysticism, but also his own deeply experienced faith. One of his contemporaries, Jusepe Martínez, wrote of him following his death: "He gave his soul to God and was so venerated that he was held almost as a saint; he sought no advantages in this life but was always honorable in his dealings; he was deeply mourned by the whole city and its inhabitants, who gave him an honorable burial." This was no small accomplishment in the Spain of the Inquisition. (Turner 1996, 26:299ff)

Tarrant, Margaret Winifred (1888-1959) – a prolific English illustrator who created posters, greeting cards, calendars, and books for fifty years. She was the only child of Percy Tarrant, a successful landscape painter as well as an illustrator for magazines, books, and greeting cards. Most popular during the 1920s and 1930s for her romantic depiction of children, fairies, and animals, Tarrant worked in many media: pen-and-ink, delicately colored watercolor, and graphite. Her silhouette drawings were also very popular. She illustrated dozens of children's books, including editions of *Alice in Wonderland*, *Mother Goose Nursery Tales*, *Hans Andersen Stories for Children*, and *The Pied Piper of Hamelin*. Tarrant exhibited at the Royal Academy and the Royal Society of Artists in Birmingham, England. According to Tarrant: "My love of nature has led me to the kind of work I do – I want to lead people's thoughts from nature's wonder to nature's Creator." (Ortakales 1999, online)

Veronese, Paolo (1528-1588) – born Paolo Caliari; called "Il Veronese," the Veronan, because of his birth in the city of Verona. A talented painter exuberant in his use of color, he specialized in both classical and religious works. He is particularly well known for his religious feast scenes, including *Supper at Emmaus*, *The Marriage at Cana*, and *Feast in the House of the Pharisee*. His depictions were sometimes more secular than religious, showing the down-to-earth humanity of his subjects. He delighted in lavish and sometimes humorous detail to such an extent that he was called to defend himself before the Inquisition when it was decided that some of the details in his painting, *Feast in the House of Levi*, were not sufficiently reverent. His defense failed, and he was forced to make changes in the painting to remove the offensive illustrations. (*New Columbia Encyclopedia*, 4th ed.)

Zeigler, Lee Woodward (1865-1952) – mural painter and illustrator, born in Baltimore, Maryland. Known especially for his murals depicting religious, historical, literary, and narrative subjects, he studied at the Maryland Institute School of Art. From 1889-1904, he drew for *Life* magazine, then began a focus on illustrations for historical novels. Director of the St. Paul School of Art in Minnesota from 1910 to 1918, Zeigler returned to Baltimore in 1918. By 1930, Zeigler's art was in great demand by universities, libraries, museums, and many churches, including Calvary Church, Cincinnati. His major, twelve-year project was *The Faerie Queen*, an eighteen-panel mural depicting the age of chivalry and covering 1,800 square feet of wall space at the Enoch Pratt Free Library in Baltimore. (Falk 1999, 3:3678ff)

altar of repose – An altar located away from the main altar on which the consecrated elements are placed following the stripping of the altar on Maundy Thursday. It is the focus for prayer and meditation during a vigil kept until the Good Friday service.

Apocrypha – An appendix to the Bible of fourteen books that are uncanonical to Protestants and rejected in Judaism, ten of which are accepted in the Roman Catholic canon.

Associates – Women and men who are associated with a religious community in prayer and service. They follow a personal Rule of Life, which is adapted to their individual circumstances, and they proclaim the Good News of God in Christ by word and example.

aspergill – A tube with a handle and perforations at one end. It is used to sprinkle holy water, an action called asperges that signifies baptismal renewal.

carillon – A set of at least twenty-three and up to seventy bells with chromatic intervals, which are played from a keyboard.

chancel – The space around the altar of a church for the choir and the celebrant.

chasuble – A long, sleeveless vestment worn by the celebrant at the Eucharist.

collect – A short prayer preceding the Eucharistic lessons that "collects" the messages of the lessons and varies with the liturgical day and season. It includes an invocation and petition and is directed to the Trinity.

cope – A long outer vestment worn by a priest on special or ceremonial occasions. It is usually richly decorated, and its color varies according to the liturgical season.

credence table – A small table holding the bread and wine before Consecration during the Eucharist.

crosier – A staff, often shaped like a shepherd's crook, carried by a bishop, abbot, or abbess and symbolizing the caretaker of the flock.

cruciform church - A church built in the form of a cross.

dalmatic – A wide-sleeved, knee-length vestment worn by an ordained person serving as a deacon during a Solemn High Eucharist.

F.A.G.O. – Fellow of American Guild of Organists. A certification from the American Guild of Organists issued to organists after a series of exams.

fair linen – The linen covering the top of the altar and hanging down over both sides.

flue voicer – An expert who manipulates the mouth area of the organ pipe to give the proper sound and volume for the shape of the pipe.

frontal – An ornamental, detachable fabric or lace covering all or part of the front of an altar.

icon – An image created as a focal point of religious veneration and regarded as sacred, especially in the tradition of Eastern Churches. The painting of the icon is itself a religious act prepared for by prayer and fasting. Icons commonly represent Christ, the Blessed Virgin Mary or other saints.

knop – A decorative knob on the stem of a chalice that makes it easier to hold.

lancet window - A pointed, narrow window.

lavabo – Ceremonial washing of the celebrant's hands before the Consecration of the elements. A lavabo bowl and a lavabo towel are used.

Maltese cross – A cross with four equal arms. Each arm increases progressively as it leaves the center.

misericord – The ledge on the underside of hinged seats in choir stalls, beautifully carved to display the artist's skill and intended to provide some relief from standing during long services.

miter – The official headdress of a bishop, shaped to symbolize the tongues of fire at Pentecost.

monasticism - Christian life that is lived in community, with commitment to the pursuit of holiness through prayer, work, and vows of poverty, chastity, and obedience.

monstrance – A decorative, cruciform receptacle with a clear glass case in its center to hold the consecrated Host for adoration.

narthex – A vestibule or room of a church between the main outside door and the main door to the nave.

nave – In a church, the large space between the narthex and the chancel. The nave is the worship space for the congregation.

office lights – Candles placed on the shelf of an altar, usually three on each side of the tabernacle.

orphreys – Ornamental bands and designs on vestments, often in elaborate embroidery.

Pantocrator – A Greek theological term meaning "ruler of the world."

piscina – A small sink used for the disposal of consecrated and blessed elements and the cleaning of their vessels. It drains directly to the ground rather than into the sewer or septic system. Usually found in the sacristy of a church.

plate tracery – The space above two lancet windows made in one arch. It is filled by a circle or quatrefoil.

prie-dieu – A kneeling bench with a raised shelf for prayer books.

quatrefoil – A leaf-like ornament having four lobes that form a cross.

reredos – The decorative structure above and behind an altar, often highly ornamented with wood or stone carving.

retable – A structure on the back of an altar, often a ledge or shelf on which ornaments may be set or a triptych.

rood – A large crucifix of Jesus in agony, located at the entrance to the chancel.

rood screen – An ornamental partition that separates the chancel from the nave. It usually has a beam supporting a crucifix.

sedilia – A set of three seats in the sanctuary intended for the use of the officiating ministers.

see – The official seat, center of authority, jurisdiction, or office of a bishop.

Theotokos Hodigitria – Greek theological terms frequently used in iconography. Theotokos means "God bearer," and Hodigitria means "directress" or "she who presents the Savior, the one to follow."

thurible – A vessel, made of brass, silver, or gold and suspended by a chain, that holds burning incense. It is used during church rituals. Also called a censer.

tonal finishing – The final adjustment of each organ pipe to produce its proper tone for the acoustics of the building.

tondo – A painting or a piece of sculpture in relief done in a circular form.

tracery – The ornamental work in the upper part of a Gothic window.

Note: All Scriptural quotations in *Chapel of the Transfiguration* are from the New Revised Standard Version of the Bible.

"Allan Crite at Home: A Tour of His House-Museum in Boston's South End," Alumni Bulletin: *Harvard Extension School*, 1998. <http://www.dce.harvard.edu/pubs/alum/1998/04.html/>

Allchin, A.M. 1958. *The Silent Rebellion: Anglican Religious Communities: 1845-1900*. London: SCM Press, Ltd.

Anson, Peter F. 1955. *The Call of the Cloister: Religious Communities and Kindred Bodies in the Anglican Communion*. London: SPCK.

"Bartolozzi," *Atlantic Monthly* 50, no. 297 (July 1883): 115-118.

Beatrice Martha, CT, Sister. 1940. *A Follower's Story*. Sister Monica Mary, CT, ed. Cincinnati: Community of the Transfiguration.

Bethany Home Chronicle. 1927-1934. Glendale, Ohio: Bethany Home School.

Bigelow, Arthur Lynds. 1948. *Carillon*. Princeton: Princeton University Press.

The Book of Common Prayer. 1928. New York: Oxford University Press.

Breiel, John H., "Song of the Carillons: J. Prower Symons, Who Plays at Bethany, Grew Up With Bells Abroad," *Cincinnati Post*, 7 February 1934.

"The Campanologists," *Time Magazine*, 7 July 1952: 64.

"Carillon Installation Blessed," *Transfiguration Quarterly* 47, no. 4 (winter 1991): 5.

Carruthers, T.H. 1965. *High on a Hill: The Story of Christ Church*, Glendale. USA.

Clarke, Charles P.S. 1968. *Everyman's Book of Saints*. Oxford: Alden Press.

Cleveland, Mrs. Harlan. 1929. *Mother Eva Mary, C.T.: The Story of a Foundation*. Milwaukee: Morehouse Publishing Co.

Cram, Ralph Adams. 1924. *Church Building: A Study of the Principles of Architecture in Their Relation to the Church*. Boston: Marshall Jones Co.

Darby, Delphine Fritz. 1938. *Francisco Ribalta and His School*. Cambridge: Harvard University Press.

Delaney, John J. 1980. *Dictionary of Saints*. New York: Doubleday and Co., Inc.

Domestici, Fiamma. 1992. *Della Robbia: A Family of Artists*. Milan: SCALA, Instituto Fotografico.

Falk, Peter Hastings, ed. 1999. *Who Was Who in American Art, 1564-1975: 400 Years of Artists in America*. 3 vols. Madison, CT: Sound View Press.

Glendale's Heritage. 1996. Cincinnati: Glendale Heritage Preservation.

Kershaw, Simon, comp. *Keeping the Feast: A Companion to the Holy Days of the Calendar 2000*. <http://oremus.org/liturgy/etc/ktf/>

Lang, Anton. 1930. *Reminiscences*. Munich: Knorr and Hirth.

Mariya Margaret, CT, Sister. 1979. "History of the Chapel of the Transfiguration." Glendale, Ohio: Community of the Transfiguration.

Myers, Bernard S., ed. 1969. *Dictionary of Art*. New York: McGraw-Hill.

Norden, Rudolph N. 1985. *Symbols and Their Meaning*. St. Louis: Concordia House.

"A Notable Consecration and Committal," *The Living Church*, 6 July 1929: 330-332.

Ortakales, Denise. 1999. "Margaret Winifred Tarrant." *Women Children's Book Illustrators*. <http://ortakales.com//Illustrators/Tarrant.html>

Plowe, Mary Lillian. 1997. "History of the Chapel of the Transfiguration." Glendale, Ohio: Community of the Transfiguration.

The Proper for the Lesser Feasts and Fasts 1997: Together with the Fixed Holy Days. 1998. New York: Church Publishing Inc.

Quenot, Michael. 1991. *The Icon: Window on the Kingdom*. Crestwood, NY: St. Vladimir's University Press.

Ruth Magdalene, CT, Sister. "Again – The Bells," *Transfiguration Quarterly* 7, no. 3 (autumn 1950). 8-19.

Ruth Magdalene, CT, Sister. "Bells," *Transfiguration Quarterly* 7, no 4 (winter 1949). 12-13.

Ruth Magdalene, CT, Sister. "Community Notes," *Transfiguration Quarterly* 8, no. 4 (winter 1951). 11.

Ruth Magdalene, CT, Sister. "More About the Bells," *Transfiguration Quarterly* 7, no. 2 (summer 1950). 16.

Ruth Magdalene, CT, Sister. "Of Carillons: The Blessing of Bells," *Transfiguration Quarterly* 8, no. 3 (autumn 1951). 6-9.

Ruth Magdalene, CT, Sister. "Our Singing Tower," *Transfiguration Quarterly* 8, no. 2 (summer 1951). 2-4.

Specifications for the Transfiguration Chapel. 1927. Boston: Cram and Ferguson, Architects.

Strychasz, Jennifer. 1998. "Allan Rohan Crite." *Exhibition: Narratives of African American Art and Identity: The David C. Driskell Collection*. The Art Gallery, University of Maryland. <http://www.inform.umd.edu/EdRes/Colleges/ARHU/Depts/ArtGal/. WWW/exhibit/98-99/driskell/exhibition/sec3/crit_a_01.htm>

Thurston, Herbert, S.J. and Donald Attwater, eds. 1956. *Butler's Lives of the Saints*. 4 vols. New York: P.J. Kennedy and Sons.

Turner, Jane, ed. 1996. *Grove Dictionary of Art*. 34 vols. London: Macmillan.

Webber, F.R. 1971. *Church Symbolism: An Explanation of the More Important Symbols of the Old and New Testament, the Primitive, the Medieval and the Modern Church*. Detroit: Gale Research Company.

Whone, Herbert. 1977. *Church Monastery Cathedral: A Guide to the Symbolism of the Christian Tradition*. Short Hills, NJ: Ridley Enslow Publishers.

Wild, Doris. 1961. *Holy Icons in the Religious Art of the Eastern Church*. Berne: Hallwag, Ltd.

Page numbers in italics refer to photographs of paintings. For other photos, see Illustrations on pages vi-vii. All Sisters listed are members of the Community of the Transfiguration unless otherwise designated.